# FROM TAKE-OFF TO TOUCHDOWN

## MY FIFTY YEARS OF FLYING

AN ILLUSTRATED AUTOBIOGRAPHY

BY

TONY FARRELL, DFC, AFC

**CIRRUS ASSOCIATES**

PUBLISHED BY:
Cirrus Associates (S.W.),
Kington Magna,
GILLINGHAM,
Dorset,
SP8 5EW UK.

## ISBN 1 902807 01 4

PRINTED IN ENGLAND BY:
The Book Factory,
35-37 Queensland Road,
LONDON,
N7 7AH.

PHOTO SCANNING BY:
Castle Graphics Ltd,
Nunney,
NR. FROME,
Somerset,
BA11 4LW.

DISTRIBUTORS:
Cirrus Associates (S.W.),
Kington Magna,
GILLINGHAM,
Dorset,
SP8 5EW.

COVER PHOTOS:
FRONT: Squadron Leader Tony Farrell, DFC, AFC, briefs a Burmese student, Maung Ki Tin, in an Avro Anson I.
Photo: by courtesy of the Ministry of Defence, © Crown Copyright/ MOD.
REAR: Tony Farrell in Hornet Moth G-ADMM at Ramsgate, 1936.
Photo: from the author's collection.

# DEDICATION

I doubt if this book would, or could, have been written without the love and support I have had from my wife Jean and my family. Jean especially, for not only – so far – 58 years of putting up with me, but also for taking on someone besotted with flying, which she hated. We first met when she was one and I was two – not that either of us remember it! Sixteen years elapsed before we met again. She was piloted by me but once (after the war) and never repeated the experience! So all power to her elbow, as they say, and my love.

# CONTENTS

# PREFACE

Now that I am an octogenarian and still (just about!) in fairly full command of my brain and its associated memories, I have decided to put on record, more or less, the story of my life as an aeroplane pilot which, starting in 1936, has lasted some 50 years.

It has covered vast changes in aviation and has given me a very fulfilled and happy career, for which I am humbly grateful. Had I put some of this on record when younger I could have, quite justifiably, been considered a hell of a line-shooter, something up to now that I have wanted to avoid. So please bear with me if the first person singular occurs so frequently; it is the trademark of any autobiography, and I hope, especially for those born since the 1970s, that they can get some idea of what an ordinary pilot's life in peace and war was like from so long ago.

# CHAPTER 1
# TAKE-OFF
## PREWAR PILOT 1936-1938

I was hooked on flying from the earliest memories I can go back to. We lived two miles from Manston aerodrome in Thanet, and as a toddler I remember going there, in a pony and trap, and stopping on the public road that went across the landing area in those days to watch the flying. I can vividly recall the "Hucks Starters" starting up the Bristol Fighters of No. 2 (Army Co-operation) Squadron stationed there. (A "Hucks Starter" was an open Ford chassis equipped with an external drive shaft that fitted into the airscrew hub.)

Later I recall quite vividly the bright red Avro 504Ks of the Cornwall Aviation Company giving 5/– joyrides to Margate holidaymakers from very small fields; with later knowledge I would have been even more impressed, especially with their slipping turns, fish-tailing and 'blipping' Clerget (or were they Le Rhône?) rotary engines! I remember one registered G-EBIZ and they frequently flew very low. My late father took a pot-shot at one with his air rifle as it just topped the trees in our garden, and on another occasion, when one flew low over our school sports field the sports master tried to knock up a tennis ball at it! After more than 70 years these memories are as clear as if they were last week. As a young boy on a school outing to Manston, I was given a taxi ride in a Vickers Virginia night bomber of No. 500 (County of Kent) heavy bomber Squadron.

The school playing field had other appropriate memories for me. I was a weekly boarder of all things, so every Monday morning was hell and every Friday afternoon bliss. It was a wonderful place to fly model aeroplanes. I don't suppose there are many now who remember the elastic-driven Warnford models. They had to be wound up laboriously by hand (as much as possible without snapping the elastic!) and though they could take off, hand-launching was better. Balsa wood was not heard of then. The wings were thin ply covered in silk and the fuselage just an ordinary square shaped stick really. The wings were held on with elastic, the tail fin & rudder and tailplane with light wire. There were three different sizes, 5/–, 10/– and 21/6 for a larger twin elastic job. They didn't last long but flew quite well if carefully adjusted. A good landing was a rarity.

Later a more sophisticated elastic flyer called a FROG (From Rise Off Ground) was developed with a box-winding mechanism, but although it flew quite well it crashed almost always and it was not all that robust. But these were good fun; they were the Blériots and Deperdussins to the modern radio-controlled wonderful replicas of today!

As I got into early teenagehood, I also began making models from crude wooden kits made by a firm called Skybirds. These were good fun and could be hand-crafted and painted to be quite accurate models.

At 13 I was sent away to boarding school, Malvern. Flying took a long pause – I never saw a plane whilst I was there – but there was a school rule that flying was prohibited. One senior had some years previously hired a Moth from a nearby club (Pershore I think) and beat up the school – hence the rule! I had to be content with reading all I could.

A well-known flying magazine called *"Popular Flying"* was excellent reading, with lots of autobiographical chapters from the aviators of the '14-'18 War. W.E. Johns (author of Biggles) was the best known.

But twice I did get to go on a day out to go with a school group to the wonderful Hendon Air Displays of '34 and '35, mouth-watering experiences for an avid young worshipper: formation, inverted formation, aerobatics, the new types coming into service and a few '14-'18 types (the Sopwith Triplane's rate of climb was phenomenal). Little did I know that one of the inverted formation pilots, Sgt. Stratton as he then was, would be Wing Commander Stratton AFC, my chief Flying Instructor at Hamble 15 years or so later. Also, little did I know that Malvern would be taken over in the war to house the radar establishment and that I would share a flat with a colleague there.

By the time I left school to work in London, an airfield had been opened at Ramsgate by the Straight Corporation, only a short bicycle ride from my home. I saved all I could and sold all my saleable possessions (except for my push-bike) to pay for lessons.

My first flight was in 1935 as passenger in a DH Dragon from Ramsgate to Le Zoute (en route to Brussels to stay with a Belgian friend) and back. My second was a 10-minute joyride in a Monospar.

Up to the time I had my first flight in the DH Dragon in 1935 I had often wondered what flying was really like. Apart from the fascination of seeing the Earth from above (in its miniature state, so to speak, everything looked so small) it did not seem to rate much as an experience. There was good weather on that day and no turbulence (or 'bumps' as we used to call it) and no sensation of speed; that surprised me most.

However, later on, as I began lessons, especially in spinning and aerobatics, there were sensations aplenty. All these eventually became part of my enjoyment of flying. But I rarely ever had to do any really low flying (or 'hedge-hopping' as we used to call it in those far-off days) and I was certainly thankful that it was not a part of my career in the RAF later on. Being completely detached from *terra firma* lessens any sense of the vertigo or panic that one sometimes gets when peering over a steep cliff or similar.

By April 1936 I had saved enough to start lessons at weekends in the club's Hornet Moth (G-ADMM); they cost £2 per hour dual and 30/– (£1.50) solo. A missed approach therefore cost about two shillings and sixpence (half-a-crown, or 12$^1$/2p today) but that I sometimes could not afford, so it sharpened judgement! I had at least three instructors; the first was the Club/Airport Manager, Charles Eckersley-Maslin, who died only recently aged 96. He was a real character, having served in the Army in 1916 until it was discovered he was under age (15) and so was probably sent back to school! He later joined the RAF and then the Rhodesian Police. In the '39-'45 War he went into the Fleet Air Arm and became a Commander (sorry if I digress).

I was sent solo after 10 hrs 20 mins dual and I remember I did a ground loop on landing, and in fact in the early days I made several bouncy landings, but things eventually 'clicked' and I got my 'A' Licence (equivalent to the present Private Pilot's Licence) in July after 11 hrs 50 mins dual and 2 hrs 50 mins solo. For the tests the aircraft had a barograph fitted; you then climbed to 2,000 feet, closed the throttle and had to land without the use of the engine to within about 50 yards from the airfield circle. (In those days all airfields had a white circle in the middle – runways did not come into use until later.) Strangely, I did not do as well as I had hoped; I passed that test OK on the 1st July 1936, but I failed the second test, which was (if I remember correctly) to carry out five or six figures of eight around the field, not above 600 feet, and then land (with use of engine if necessary) as close as possible to the circle. The barograph showed that I had exceeded the maximum height. It is worth remembering that these tests were designed for the less reliable and unsophisticated aircraft of pre-1914 vintage and also there were no sensitive-type altimeters in our light aircraft in those days: calibrations were at 200-foot intervals and quite close together.

The next day, July the 2nd, I took my father's car to Canterbury and passed the driving test, and the day after that I retook and passed the figure-of-eight test – phew! So 'A' Licence No. 9968 and Royal Aero Club Aviator's Certificate No. 14011 were issued to me. I retained No. 9968 on all my subsequent civil licences, but the Royal Aero Club Certificate was more impressive: it bore a ghastly photograph of me and instructions in several languages (including Russian) to help me if needed! (See Appendix 1.)

Meanwhile I was still bouncing about on landings; eventually I got it consistently right, but I dread to think how I would have fared on an RAF course. At Ramsgate they were awfully tolerant towards me!

My second type solo was on the 1st November 1936 in the Kronfeld Drone G-AEEN (24 hp Carden Ford engine – the registration was apt, it sounded like that at full throttle!). It had to be solo, it only had one seat! Later on I had quite an interesting experience in G-AEEN. I was flown up to Hanworth (South London) and asked to bring the Drone back to Ramsgate (it had had an overhaul up there, I think). Anyway, on the 10th June 1937 I flew it from Hanworth to Ramsgate against a very stiff headwind and the 60-odd mile journey took me 1 hour and 55 minutes to complete. I had the humiliation of being overtaken by a Southern Railways train on the long straight from Redhill to Ashford!

On the 14th November 1936 I did my first cross-country to Lympne – no dual cross-countries in those days! – and on the 22nd November 1936 I had an 'experience'! My then instructor, Leslie Mouatt (who had sent me on my first solo the previous July) had to deliver an aircraft to Lympne – would I like to fly down in the Hornet and bring him back? – would I just! I took off soon after him but never saw him; the weather closed in and I stooged about below low cloud and in poor visibility, quite lost, so I gave up and got back to Ramsgate worried sick at abandoning him at Lympne. But, of course, as I taxied in, a very worried Leslie Mouatt greeted me with enormous relief. With his extra experience he had not pressed on – an excellent safety lesson for me.

On the 13th January 1937 my third type was an all-silver Cirrus Swallow, G-AERK, a lovely easy comfortable monoplane with a large windscreen (so helmet not really necessary), and I remember later on clocking up my 100th hour solo in her. The fourth type was a Hillson Praga G-AEPI in February 1937, and the fifth a Taylor J/2 Cub, G-AESK. I had logged 17 hours 25 minutes dual as passenger and 20 hours 30 minutes solo at the end of my first year of flying.

In my second year sundry other types came my way; the most notable was on the 6th June 1937 when I had 15 minutes in the little single-seater Tipsy S.2 monoplane G-AEWJ (24 hp Sprite engine). I was promised a second flight in it that afternoon, but tragically it was not to be, as it was thoroughly 'pranged' by someone else. I don't remember the pilot's name, nor if he survived, but he was (as we called it) 'stunting' and he crashed in a field next to the aerodrome. My camera caught him being pulled out of the wreckage – tragic. My next type was a Gipsy Moth on 28th July 1937 – G-ABPK.

I had an ambition to find out how high our club aircraft could go. I tested three: the Hornet Moth G-ADMM got me up to 18,000 ft on the 25th June 1937 (a total flight time of 1 hour 15 minutes), and on the 21st of August that year the BA Swallow G-AERK reached 19,000 ft. On the 10th April 1938 I got our brand-new Miles Magister G-AFEU up to 21,000 feet: 52 minutes to get there and eight minutes to get back down. This took 5 gallons of fuel to achieve, not a bad fuel consumption. The altitude control was used above 6,000 ft. Of course in those days we did not have sensitive altimeters; height was calibrated in 200 ft marks not very far apart, so accuracy was doubtful. Nevertheless the Earth looked very small and in the open cockpit Swallow and "Maggie" it was COLD! (For my performance graphs drawn at the time, see Appendix 2.)

On the 24th July I had a marvellous day out. I was asked by the owner of Swallow G-AERK, dear old "Uncle Albert" Batchelor, if I would accompany his niece Gladys, the Air Queen of Rochester, on a flight down to Roborough, Plymouth, as she had been entered in the Devon Air Day race. (Things were easier in those days. I didn't even know if she was qualified. I never remember her flying solo – I think I was nominally in charge! Anyway, she always let me do most of the flying when we flew together.)

We had an early start. The first leg was to Eastleigh to refuel – with strong headwinds, it took us 2 hours. Eastleigh to Exeter took 1 hour 20 minutes, and Exeter to Plymouth 30 minutes; we got there 30 minutes before the deadline! The actual race took us 1 hour 5 minutes on a triangular course: Plymouth–Haldon–Exeter–Plymouth. Our average speed was 88 mph (no knots in those days) and we were last but one! Last were the radio singing brothers (actually I believe they were cousins) Kenneth and George Weston, also in a Swallow. The race was won by a cunning ex-RFC pilot (Phillips I think his name was) in an Avro 504, possibly G-ADBR, who got as high as he could on the first leg to get maximum advantage of the tailwind.

It was hellish rough on the last leg from Exeter to Plymouth, low flying over Dartmoor into the strong headwind. It was some small consolation that our average speed for the race was some 7.25 mph faster than the Western Brothers' Swallow's speed of 80.75 mph. Afterwards we flew back via another refuelling stop at Exeter, taking 2 hours 40 minutes to get home, a day's total of 7 hours 35 minutes – a memorable day out in every way.

At this stage perhaps it would be appropriate to mention three 'social' events connected with Ramsgate airport.

The first big day was the Flying Flea Race on 3rd August 1936. (Some details from the Programme are given in Appendix 3.) Fleas were incredible little buzzers, and to me and many other inexperienced pilots vastly tricky, almost dangerous – as they soon proved to be, being very unstable in pitch and the cause of many a prang. I don't believe that they would ever be allowed a C. of A. (Certificate of Airworthiness) in this modern day. The noise of their high-revving engines made wasps as jealous as hell! I must admit, however, that Henri Mignet himself (the inventor) was a tremendous character – the French word *élan* describes him – and his handling of his cabin version of the Pou-du-Ciel was masterly. The winner of the race was a Frenchman called Bret.

The second major event was the official opening of the airport on 3rd July 1937 by the Director General of Civil Aviation, Lt. Col. Sir Francis Shelmerdine. As a member I got an excellent free lunch (see Appendix 4) and a close look at a lot of interesting civil and military aircraft. A very unusual one was the Horden-Richmond small twin (designed for the Duke of Richmond and Gordon of Goodwood fame). It had no rudder bar; the elevators and ailerons worked as normal on the control column and yaw was also made on it by moving a handlebar on top to the left or right as needed. It never caught on and I can well understand why!

The third major event at the airport took place on Saturday the 21st August 1937. The Thanet Air Race was an exciting competition between 18 assorted types from Great Britain and Europe including three Germans and a most fascinating Latvian VEF.12 flown by a man called Vitols. I wonder what happened to them all? I did a few odd jobs on that day, including painting the race number on Alex Henshaw's Mew Gull G-AEXF. The winner was Paul Elwell, demonstration pilot for Taylor Cubs, in G-AESK, second was the Spartan Arrow G-ABOB flown by H.R.A. Edwards and third was Alex Henshaw's Mew Gull. (Some details from the Programme are given in Appendix 5.)

The term VIP had not been coined in 1937, but I flew a minor one on June 19th of that year when I was asked to give a joyride to Alderman Noble, Mayor of Margate. My total solo hours at that time were 30 – I was very glad he did not know that!

On the 31st July 1937 I flew for the first time the lovely old Spartan Arrow G-ABOB (Gipsy II engine), a splendid robust biplane heavier than the Moth. On 7th August 1937 I flew the

Hillson Praga G-AEUP, but I didn't like it much; I think it was a bit underpowered with a Continental 40/50 hp engine. Next on 5th March 1938 I flew what was then called the Miles Magister G-AFEU; it was the first of many flights on that type and my first experience of what we then called 'blind flying' under the hood fitted to the rear cockpit – very claustrophobic and similar to those fitted to service Tiger Moths.

Later, on the 10th April 1938, I climbed it to 22,000 feet (on the old-type altimeter). It performed well as it was a brand-new aircraft and took me 52 minutes to go up and 8 minutes to descend – ignorance and foolhardiness but I got away with it.

About this time I applied for a Short Service Commission in the RAF, but to my consternation I was turned down by failing the medical – twice. I couldn't keep the mercury blown up long enough and was made too dizzy by the whirling chair test (presumably checking one's reaction to spinning). Strangely and fortunately when I did get into the RAF in 1939 I never failed another medical until my final retirement in 1984, but I never failed to worry about it. I suppose that, with hindsight, if I had passed that first one and had been given a Short Service Commission my changes of survival would have been considerably reduced! But it's quite a thought when one's career depends on medicals twice a year.

In June 1938 we had one of the first Miles Whitney Straights, G-AFBV, and I enjoyed several hours on it, but I preferred the Hornet Moths. Sometimes when our instructor Leslie Mouatt flight-tested the Hornet he took his Alsatian dog up with him; it was quite impressive to see him sitting up and enjoying the view from the right-hand seat. I had a dog called Daniel (a cross between a dog and a spaniel!) and I let him sit on the luggage platform behind the seats and fixed his collar to the straps. He behaved but was probably bored.

I once saw Mouatt take off in a strong wind in the Taylorcraft and climb to 1,000 feet to the upwind end of the field; he took it to the point of stall on full flap and full throttle and allowed the aircraft to drift backwards to the downwind end, then throttle back and glide in! I've never been able to do it, the best I've managed is an into-wind hover!

I met with an aircraft at Hanworth in 1938 that I have never seen a trace of since the war, and that was the Blackburn B.2. It was being used in a film called "In the Air," featuring George Formby (the ukelele-playing comic) and Polly Ward. Hanworth in South London was a somewhat unusual airfield as the main hangars and offices were in the centre of the airfield.

The Blackburn was a basic trainer like the Tiger with, I believe, the same engine, but had side-by-side seating. I was most disappointed never to get to fly one. There was a lot of argument at the time between the protagonists of tandem versus side-by-side seating. The arguments were fairly finely balanced, in my opinion. One thing in favour of side-by-side was that the instructor could set a clearer example of handling and cockpit management to the student, and it was a little easier to survey the student from the corner of one's eye as to how his reactions and control handling were used.

A chapter on prewar flying would not be complete without a mention of the many free passenger flights that I enjoyed almost as much as doing the actual handling. One quite memorable occasion was on Empire Air Day in 1937 when I was flown over to Manston in Dragon G-AECZ by the airport manager (and my first flying instructor), Captain Charles Eckersley-Maslin. It was a thrilling day out for me, seeing the latest RAF aircraft such as the Gloster Gladiator and the Avro Anson. On that day I was given a lift back to Ramsgate by none other than Whitney Straight himself (owner of Ramsgate) in a Percival Gull G-ADFA, forerunner of the Proctor.

Manston and Ramsgate were only five minutes apart, a situation that would be greeted with horror, I believe, in this day and age!

We also used at Ramsgate a small twin called a Short Scion, G-ADDV, with two Pobjoy engines; it was used for joyrides and occasional parachute-drops. I went up in it when a Mr Hine did a jump, a most interesting experience. (Throughout my RAF service I was very glad I never had to use the parachute I had to sit on!). Another nice little twin was the DH Dragonfly G-ADNA.

The 1st July 1938 was another memorable day for me as I flew to Lympne and after a dual check did my first solo in a Tiger Moth, G-ADWG. Little did I then realise that I would clock up nearly

2,000 hours on the type. Then on the 3rd of July a first solo on a type really to revel in: the Miles (as we then called it) – or the Southern – Martlet single-seat biplane, G-AAYX, with the 90 hp Siddeley Genet Major engine, owned at that time by one Kenneth Vincent. I did three flights in this delightful little mini-fighter, now being lovingly restored by the Shuttleworth Trust at Old Warden 60 years later. May it survive to beyond the millennium! July also saw my first solo on Puss Moth G-ABWZ.

The Taylor Cub G-AFFJ was an interesting example of an unusual modification I have never ever seen again – I flew it for 15 minutes at Hanworth on June 14th. It had a single-blade propeller and a counterweight on the opposite side. The slower the speed the finer the pitch of the single blade (it oscillated on its hub in some strange manner), theoretically therefore having a lower drag benefit and an automatic pitch. I have never, ever, seen anything like it since: it seemed a brilliant idea to me.

In November 1938, shortly after my 21st birthday, my firm sent me to St. Vincent in the Cape Verde Islands (a Portuguese possession), about 400 miles west of the bulge in Africa and just north of the Equator, as a ship's coaling clerk. It was very aptly described by an American ship's captain as "Half the size of New York Cemetery and twice as dead!" So I departed with a heavy heart, braced by the experience of what I thought as my last flight.

On the 24th of November, the day before I sailed, I arranged to meet a friend on the green above the cliffs at Cliftonville (Margate) in Hornet Moth G-AFDT. I switched off and stopped the propeller to simulate a forced landing (there were very few people about, it was winter, remember) and all went well, my first (as we called it then) 'dead stick landing.'

We met and said goodbye, I started up (hand-swing of course) and flew back to Ramsgate, taking 35 minutes, thinking I might never fly again! So ended my early years of aviation. I sailed the next day, little knowing that I would be back before the end of 1939 and that my last log book entry would be chuckled over by the RAF officers who reviewed my application to join up when I got back soon after the outbreak of war.

To sum up: 52.05 hours dual/passenger, 123.30 hours solo and 14 types but, best of all, terrific memories and nostalgia.

CHAPTER 2

# IN THE HOLDING PATTERN

### EXILE TO CAPE VERDE ISLANDS 1938-1939

When I left school I joined a firm of General Merchants and Coal exporters in the City of London. For three years I worked as a clerk in the various departments for a pittance, but there were advantages – I managed to earn enough to learn to fly, had most weekends free and, most important of all, met the lovely girl (for the second time, I was two and she was one year old at our first meeting but neither of us remember it!) who eventually decided, after a long sustained effort by me, that life with me was bearable – but that comes later!

I lived in digs in Hampstead and commuted by train to my home at weekends. The line crossed over the river Medway at Rochester and I used to look for the Short flying boats moored in the river by their factory, including the "Maia" and "Mercury" combination used for experimental long-distance flights.

In due course I was 'kitted out' and sent as a coaling clerk to the firm's coaling depot at São Vicente (St. Vincent as we called it) in the Cape Verde Islands.

St. Vincent had hardly any vegetation (all the trees except one had been felled years before) and no water. This had to be imported in barges from a neighbouring island, Santo Antão, about 10 miles away. But it did possess a large magnificent sheltered deep-water anchorage. The inhabitants were descendants of slaves dumped there during the slave trade. They were pitiably poor and undernourished. There were a dozen or so Portuguese administrators and around 50 English (including four or five brave wives), who ran the coaling depot, the telegraph station and the Shell oil depot.

In those days merchant ships from Europe burning coal had space in their bunkers for enough to reach South America and back as far as St. Vincent, where coal was much cheaper than in

Argentina, Uruguay or Brazil. Our firm exported coal from South Wales and Durham and stocked it at St. Vincent.

There was no harbour as such, just one short quay. Ships anchored in the bay and coal was taken out in lighters, towed by a small steam tug, and a squad of natives filled sacks with coal which were hoisted on board by the ship's derricks. It was a filthy job, coal dust got everywhere and we had to wear a white tropical uniform! There was constant war and bickering between most ships' chief engineers and the coaling clerks as to the average weight of each coal bag, so that the total tonnage uptake could be calculated. Each sack hoisted on board had to be counted by a tally clerk, in turn supervised by one of the ships' crew. To load, say, 200 tons – an average weight – took anything up to six hours. Eight sacks per ton meant that 1,600 bags had to be emptied into the ship's bunkers. But it was challenging and very interesting!

I still remember Captain Nedelcu and his charming wife of the Romanian ship "*Oltul*," Captain Hillen of the Dutch tramp "*Bussum*" and of course there were English, Greek, German, Swedish, Norwegian and several other nationalities. I coaled a lot of Greek ships and even learned to count in Greek for that reason. They also made the best Turkish coffee, with which they were generous in supplying us.

We signalled to the shore, when necessary, with flags. I think the most dangerous moment in my life occurred there when I had to climb down a rope ladder over the side of a tramp ship at night when ready to go ashore, absolutely tight after being regaled with some sort of ghastly alcohol by a friendly captain! To this day I don't know why I didn't fall off into the filthy water below.

When we got ashore we were as black as the Ace of Spades with coal dust and utterly exhausted. Water was strictly rationed on the island; baths were rare, but we had showers. It was a three-year posting, followed by a few months' leave, then probably to Brazil, Uruguay or Argentina; but the war intervened and I resigned in November 1939 to get back to join up.

Life on the island was very basic – we did have a golf course, but the 'greens' were sand and fuel oil mixed to give a surface on which one could putt. We had a local rule that one's caddie was allowed to smooth a path with his bare foot from the ball to the hole!

Three of us coaling clerks clubbed together and got an old Humber tourer sent out from the UK so we could get out from the 'town,' called Mindelo. A driving test was necessary, and it involved giving the Portuguese Gobernador a ride around the town. I am still in possession of my Portuguese driving licence, and it was far more impressive than my flying licences!

Food was of very poor quality – I do not even recall any decent fish. Occasionally we bought or scrounged food, including bread, from the ships we coaled. Anything imported from the UK was very expensive and very little of it was available. In the eleven months I was there I think we had only three or four days' rain. A small local steamer used to ply between the seven or so islands of the group but we never had an opportunity to use it.

One of the traditions the firm had was an egg-eating competition – all newcomers to the firm had to undergo it. The record stood at 24 when I was made to attack it, and I broke the record with 29. Mind you, I had been working a very long day without a meal and deliberately got hungry, and the eggs there were smaller than the ones we know in the UK. They had to be poached, fried or boiled (I had them in alternate batches of four, the 28th and last I drank virtually raw!). Omelettes and scrambled were not allowed as counting was not possible. I suffered no ill effects, even the next morning when I went out in the tug to coal a ship and we passed the floating body of a drowned native on the way!

When the war came my dilemma could be well-imagined; I was desperate to get back. On one occasion I was coaling a Greek tramp (neutral at that time) when four crew rowed over from a large Panamanian tanker. It was actually a German ship under a flag of convenience – Portugal being neutral of course – and there was I, an Englishman, talking to four Germans on neutral territory (Greece)! They wanted news of the war and asked (in vain) for a chance to get back to Europe. We were formally polite to each other!

Soon after this I was coaling the Dutch ship *"Bussum,"* which I had coaled before, and mentioned to the captain, who was friendly, my dilemma about wanting to get back.

He said: "How long are you going to take to finish the coaling?"

"About four hours," I replied.

"OK, then you have four hours to make your mind up!"

I signalled ashore for the tug to come out, went ashore and saw the manager and resigned, packed, took the tug back to the ship and left St. Vincent for ever; God! I was well out of it.

I had an uneventful journey home – it took about ten days, I think. I slept in a small single cabin under the bridge, fed with the Captain, the Mate and the Chief Engineer, painted Dutch flags on the hatches in the morning and took an afternoon watch as helmsman, NE by N 52° (I even remember it in Dutch!), but I got slack and the Mate bawled me out for the unsteady curving wake astern of the dear old *"Bussum"*!

We anchored in the contraband control area just off Ramsgate (a short bus ride from my home) but I did not know about this and expected to disembark in Holland. When the inspectors came aboard I asked them if I could come ashore and they raised no objection. I went to the Captain to thank him and asked what I owed him.

"Nothing," he answered, "but give the steward something for the food you've eaten!"

So I gave him £5, not bad for a 2,000-odd-mile journey. I went ashore in the inspector's motor boat and home with all my bits and pieces by taxi (this was the 'phoney war', December 1939), much to my parents' surprise.

I went up to London the next day and set about getting into the RAF. They were not recruiting for pilots at the time, but I was told that if I could prove I had been a member of the Civil Air Guard I would be accepted. I rushed around and found their office, and they gave me the necessary evidence. (I had joined the organisation prewar as they gave very cheap flying.) I passed the entry interview at Uxbridge and (to my intense relief) the medical, and in December 1939 No. 908983 AC2 A. W. Farrell was sworn in to the RAF Volunteer Reserve.

At last!

CHAPTER 3
# STRAIGHT AND LEVEL
## BACK TO FLY 1939-1942

On the 8th December 1939 I passed my joining interview at RAF No. 1 Reception Centre, Uxbridge. No trouble with the medical, thank God.

I had been very worried indeed about the medical (which you may remember I failed in 1937 when applying for a Short Service Commission). I cannot bear to think what life would have been like for me if I had not passed this one, although in civil aviation they were frequent – every six months – when one held a commercial licence.

Two memories of the short time I was there: queuing up stripped to the waist, left arm on hip, for inoculations (tough Australians fainting!) and working in the cookhouse scouring out vats of tea, emptying one half-full into a second to discover that gravy and tea were being mixed. The sergeant in charge was highly amused when he found out what had been done.

"Don't worry," he said, "they'll never know the difference."

On New Year's Day we all moved out to No. 1 ITW (Initial Training Wing) at Cambridge. I was billeted with several pals (mostly Australian) in Pembroke College. We dined in Hall with the students and relaxed (when we had the chance) in the lovely secluded college precincts, the backs and the town. It was bitterly cold at that winter. We had to set out our kit at the bottom end of our stripped beds and my damp flannel froze to the metal bedstead at the foot of mine. There were compensations: we were soon promoted to Leading Aircraftsmen (L A/C) with a corresponding pay increase (from memory up from 2/- to 3/6 per day), but of course it was 'all found' food and shelter.

We passed the time in classrooms, learning elementary navigation, meteorology, air gunnery, etc., went for quite a lot of route marches, including Grantchester, and learned drilling on the town's car parks. Our Flight Sergeant in charge was a super character by the name of Harrall, later promoted to Warrant Officer.

Although drill was not new to me (I had been in the Officer's Training Corps at school) I once made a stupid mistake in a drill, and he publicly bawled me out in a very loud voice:

"If the brains in your head were gunpowder there wouldn't be enough to blow your cap badge off!"

Somebody else was called a "filleted earwig." Oh! happy but frustrating days – we were all eager to see an aeroplane.

We also had guard duties at 'our' entrance to Pembroke. The undergraduates used a different one and we did not mix apart from meal times in Hall.

Then, suddenly, we were all moved out on the 21st May and we found ourselves, after a long boring train journey, billeted in the town hall of Falkirk, of all places. We went out to the airfield there at night for guard duties and I remember sitting in a Boulton Paul Defiant and wondering what it was like to fly. (It turned out to be useless apparently!) We were only there for six days and joy, oh! joy, I travelled south again, posted to No. 10 EFTS (Elementary Flying Training School) at a little gem of a grass airfield at Yatesbury in Wiltshire.

There followed three weeks of aviation bliss – I had a nice instructor (Sergeant Jones) – and I wondered how rusty my flying was going to be after an 18-month gap, but after a not-too-straight take-off everything else was OK and there was no trouble with the landing.

Had I been wealthy I would have willingly paid the earth for that course, but it was all for free! All the aerobatics you could think of, cross-countries, forced landings in fields; even the ground school was interesting and practical. I prayed for a posting to fighters. I got an above-average assessment but a posting to No. 3 SFTS (Service Flying Training School) not far up the road, so to speak, at South Cerney near Cirencester, on Airspeed Oxfords. I was bitterly disappointed, but perhaps the survival prospects were a little less grim – not that we gave much, if any, thought to that sort of thing; but I did not relish bombers.

I reported on the 18th June and started under Flt. Lt. Fisher (of Christchurch fame). My instructor was a Flying Officer Zweigbergk, a South African. He was a good instructor, calm and reassuring. The Oxford was not an easy aircraft – it could swing badly on take-off if not very carefully controlled – but an excellent trainer, as the service types one continued on later were generally not so difficult (under normal conditions).

South Cerney was the first prewar RAF airfield I was posted to, and what a revelation it was. I had a room to myself in the Officer's Mess and shared a batman: the food was marvellous. Most of us on the course were prewar members of the RAFVR; many already had wings and were Sergeants (I was still an L A/C – we were in a minority). Even so some of the Sergeants did not get through the course. It lasted from May 28th 1940 until September 9th, and was divided into two parts, intermediate and advanced. I went solo after 2 hours 45 minutes.

On the 14th July I had my first dual night-flying, four landings in 55 minutes. The flare path was a very primitive line of paraffin flares, and on my second night I went solo after a total of 1 hour 10 minutes dual. From the second night on we all flew out just before sunset to our relief landing ground at Bibury. It was a large field with a barn and a hut at one end. In the wartime blackout it was a work of art not to get lost on the circuit. I did get lost later on, but that experience will be explained in due course.

Another interesting landmark for me was my first dual formation flying on the 27th July. Another student was killed in a formation collision with an Australian Sergeant Pilot Instructor (I think his name was Sly) who brought his pupil back safely with a lot of one of his wings torn off. He immediately took his pupil up in another aircraft in order to help him get over the shock and give him the incentive to carry on. I believe he got a well-deserved AFM for that.

The second (advanced) part of the course began on the 4th of August and for this we paired up with another pupil (a Sergeant Rowntree in my case, a very pleasant and competent character), and it consisted of 'bombing' by *camera obscura*, mutual instrument flying, reconnaissance of things like Swindon railway works and junction, air-to-air and air-to-ground 'shooting' with camera gun (these Oxfords had gun turrets), doing navigation for one's co-pilot and more night-flying, using an aerodrome floodlight which was switched on for a short time when on final approach. We also did practice bomb-dropping and a lot of cross-countries. Finally on September the 9th, my last day on the course, a generous Pilot Officer O'Neil, one of the staff, took me up for a ride in the back seat of a Hawker Audax (K2001) as a special treat!

I then learned that my next posting was to No. 2 FIS (Flying Instructors' School) at Cranwell, to be trained as an instructor; I had not bargained for that! I was also informed that I was now a commissioned Pilot Officer, No. 85281. This took me by surprise; I had no inkling whatsoever that I had ever been considered for a commission. Perhaps I could have guessed, because I had been put into the Officer's Mess – I thought it was due to overcrowding in the airmen's quarters! I had to request 48 hours leave to get a uniform – it was granted. I went to London, of course: Gieves did me proud.

Getting this course was unexpected. Cranwell still kept a modicum of its RAF College atmosphere. The airfield was a big grass one divided by its buildings into North and South halves. We used the North. I had a marvellous Canadian instructor, Flying Officer Mackid. I didn't exactly hate his guts, but he nagged continuously and made me resolve never, but never, to do that sort of thing. I learned that half the art was to put oneself in one's pupil's shoes and the longer one did the job the harder was it necessary to remember that. Patience, even in wartime, was the name of the game.

There were several well-known prewar instructors on the staff – Alington, Ranald Porteous, and Hackney (who had checked me out in a Tiger at Lympne in 1938). We had Oxfords and – joy! – Avro Tutors. We did not do much on the latter, but what we did was thoroughly enjoyable.

One (to me) sad sight there was a collection of half-a-dozen or so Fairey Hendon night bombers – dark green large open-cockpit machines powered, I think, by Rolls-Royce Kestrel engines. I expected they were broken up eventually, relics of a bygone age.

The course finished on the 16th October and I was given an average assessment. Total of this course was 17 hours 55 minutes dual and 27 hours 40 minutes 'solo' – solo in this case was practice with another pupil on the course. (We did not call ourselves 'students' in those days.) We had a choice of where to be posted and as I knew South Cerney (local knowledge is useful when starting work!) I elected to go back there. I was becoming productive at last, five months after starting flying in the RAF.

*"What did you do in the war, Daddy?*
*How did you help us to win?"*
*"Circuits and bumps and turns, laddie,*
*And how to get out of a spin."*

*Woe and alack and misery me,*
*I trundle around in the sky*
*And instead of machine-gunning Nazis*
*I'm teaching young hopefuls to fly.*

*Thus is my patience rewarded,*
*My years of experience paid,*
*Never a Hun have I followed right down,*
*Nor ever gone out on a raid.'*

(With acknowledgement to Owen Chave, the above are the first verses of his poem "The Flying Instructor's Lament.")

So back I went to South Cerney, and on the very first day, after a ten-minute solo air test of Oxford L9702, I began productive work at last, including giving night dual at Bibury. One averaged about 50 hours a month, and had one day off per week. (Weekends did not exist, the only difference on a Sunday was that newspapers cost 2d instead of 1d on weekdays!)

We had an excellent flight commander in Flight Lieutenant "Lofty" Edwards and a very good lot of instructors, including one Czech, Oscar Oleschuck. Night-flying at Bibury was rather more memorable than day-flying, as finding one's way around a very dimmed-out flare path was not easy. We generally had a flare path of glim lamps, and flares, no angle of approach indicator, and we used the aircraft's landing light for touchdown, although a floodlight was sometimes used. Throughout my service career I only ever had one night landing away from base, and that was when instructing at Bibury.

One night in very hazy conditions I 'lost' our flare path and flew round until I 'found' it again, and landed. Unfortunately I saw

Ansons on the ground, not Oxfords, so I realised we had landed at Little Rissington's satellite, Windrush! I took off again and did then manage to locate Bibury's beacon and get back there.

There was one very tragic happening at Bibury one night. On the 2nd June 1941 I sent L A/C Burbidge on his first night solo; I stood by the threshold and saw him make a good approach and smooth touchdown – then to my surprise he opened up and went round again. For some unaccountable reason he did not switch off his landing light and I saw it suddenly waver and plunge down into the ground. It was a horrifying thing to watch. We stopped flying and spent the rest of the night searching for the wreckage, but dawn came before we found him dead in the cockpit.

There was, of course, an enquiry. The aircraft had just come off overhaul and had had a night-flying test, the pupil was sent solo with confidence and did make a good landing. I did not see the findings of the enquiry, but it was obviously spatial disorientation, probably induced by the landing light distracting the pupil, possibly an artificial horizon failure. It was my only experience of any of my pupils crashing, but the horror remains with me. It was war – work and life went on.

Soon after this we had Poles sent for retraining after getting out of Europe. They were all strong characters, good pilots who quickly adapted to our ways, and their naked hatred of the Germans was chilling – of course, at that time they had good reasons to hate the Germans more than we did. I wonder what happened to them, including Flying Officer Kucharski and Corporals Zelazni and Skulicz?

On the 11th October 1941 I was sent on a ten-day course to No. 1 Beam Approach School at Watchfield, returning to Cerney on the 22nd. I served only four more days before being posted back to Watchfield to be an instructor there. So ended a very happy association with my first productive work of the war. I visited South Cerney 57 years later. The grass field and the hangars were still there, but the army was in possession and I was not allowed past the barrier!

At this stage it seems appropriate to recap on my existence outside the service. When I got back to the UK I quickly renewed my pursuit of Jean (when abroad we had exchanged letters), and even spent a night with her and her family in London. I think I made some sort of impression as she burnt the toast at breakfast, but still played hard to get! When I was instructing at South Cerney, I would hitch-hike to London to see her on my day off, and catch the last train – the milk train – back from Paddington to Kemble, the nearest stop to South Cerney, about three miles or so away. I remember tracing the roads by air from there to Cerney with the aid of the excellent quarter-inch maps we used at that time; but the first time I tried it ended in disaster.

I used to tip the guard on the train to let me use a first-class compartment (third-class ticket of course – second-class did not exist then) and wake me up at Kemble. Anyway on the walk back at about 3 am I must have taken a wrong turning and got hopelessly lost! Came the dawn and I found a phone box but the operator was highly suspicious and would not tell me where I was. (It has to be remembered that all signposts and place names had been removed for security reasons.) Eventually a van passed and stopped for me and I staggered into flights about 9 am (half an hour late). Lofty Edwards, my flight commander at the time, promptly sent me to bed, bless him!

On one hitch-hiking occasion I was walking up the hill on the London road out of Faringdon in Berkshire when I noticed a large slow tanker lorry grinding slowly towards me. As it was crawling so slowly I decided not to 'thumb it,' but it stopped and the driver called out: "Going to London, mate?"

When I said "Yes," he said: "So am I! Hop in," so I couldn't refuse. He was delivering a load of milk to a depot in Finchley, North London, only a short walk from Jean's home, so it was worth it!

Anyway, Jean continued to play hard to get; even her family asked her what she was playing at, so I resolved on a final desperate ploy to win her – I cut off all communication and waited. It worked! After what seemed ages I got a letter from her out of the blue, asking how I was, so we arranged to meet on my next leave, due in January 1941. I stayed at some very nice digs in Hampstead where I used to live when working in the City, and on my first free morning met her in Oxford Street. It was the 17th January 1941 and there and then I asked her to marry me when the war was over.

She said: "No! I'll marry you as soon as possible!"

So we tied the knot on the 9th August 1941 and we have never had a harsh word since! She has been a brave, loyal and wonderful wife and mother – I was even luckier than I realised at the time. After a honeymoon in Cambridge (how frequently that lovely town becomes involved in my life) I arranged some digs for us in Cirencester, and the day she was coming I got an afternoon off to meet her at the station. However being young and ardently in love I decided to hitch-hike to Swindon (about 10–12 miles down the road) and join her train there to give her a surprise. When the 1.45 from Paddington arrived I got on but couldn't find her anywhere, so I found the guard and gave her description. He told me that the train ran in two parts and the part I was on was bound for Bristol! I should have waited for the Cheltenham part. Anyway the first stop was Badminton, so I had about 20 miles to hitch back. (Few taxis and very little traffic in war time.) I don't remember how I did it, but got lifts to arrive about an hour late to find my poor new bride sitting on her luggage on the pavement outside Cirencester station. She had no idea where she was going to live, of course. She forgave me and we 'lived out' together during most of my service career – sometimes unofficially when I was on ops – and so we lived happily ever after, a fairy tale come true!

## CHAPTER 4
# BLIND FLYING
## BEAM APPROACH 1942-1944

On the 11th October 1941 I was posted to No. 1 Blind Approach School at Watchfield, near Swindon (only about ten minutes flying from South Cerney) for a ten-day instrument flying course on Oxfords and Ansons. Watchfield was a civilian-operated school; the CO, Wing Commander Jenkins, was an employee of Air Service Training. The firm moved up from Hamble: engineers and support staff remained civilians. It was a very efficiently managed unit and operated almost completely independent of weather conditions.

At this stage a word of explanation of 'Blind' – later changed to 'Beam' – approach is appropriate. It was developed from the pre-war German Lorenz radio beam used by Lufthansa. A transmitter (taking terrain and prevailing wind into account) was sited at the boundary of the airfield, sending out a 'beam' or steady continuous note along the direction of approach. Either side of the beam Morse dots and dashes gradually merged (the twilight zone) into the steady note of the beam. The user, who would know the magnetic direction of the beam, would manoeuvre his aircraft to maintain direction of approach to the runway (in earliest cases to the boundary of the grass airfield). There were two marker beacons: the outer – recognised by low-pitch dashes – about two miles from the airfield had to be crossed at 600 feet, and the inner – high-pitched dots – at 200 feet close to the threshold.

There was also a 'back beam' – usually without markers – that could be used for positioning overhead outbound. Before the war Lufthansa pilots made blind landings on this system, which was feasible with a grass field and an accurate altimeter setting to airfield pressure. Such landings were done by us at Watchfield on a few occasions: it had no runways as such. With a runway alignment to consider it was usually too critical and a missed approach had to be carried out if ground was not visible at 50 feet. Most Bomber Command airfields were equipped with it, and it did not go out of service until several years after the war, being superseded by ILS (Instrument Landing System) and GCA (Ground Controlled Approach).

Anyway I enjoyed the course, 22 hours flying and eight hours in the Link Trainer (a diabolical box of tricks and the illegitimate ancestor of the modern flight simulator!), and after only a week back at South Cerney I found myself posted back there on the staff as a 'Beam' instructor. So Jean and I moved into a dear little cottage in Faringdon, about four miles away, and I cycled daily into work.

I greatly enjoyed my time at Watchfield. I had been promoted to Flying Officer at South Cerney and became a Flight Lieutenant whilst I was at Watchfield. The atmosphere was business-like, friendly and informal and we worked a shift system. Speaking from memory I think it was four days from 08.00–13.00, four days from 13.00–18.00 and four days from 18.00 to, I think, midnight; two days off completed a two-week cycle. Day or night, it was all the same to the 'Beam.'

There were many characters both on the staff and the courses. When I was promoted to a flight commander one of my instructors was a Flight Lieutenant Maclaren, who later became Lord Aberconway, and of two students one was a Pilot Officer Wedgwood Benn, elder brother of the politician who demoted himself from the peerage. Had his elder brother survived the war I don't suppose the peerage would have lapsed. Another character was a Flight Lieutenant Foxley-Norris who rose up to the dizziest heights of ranks in the postwar service.

It was nice to have Ansons to fly as well as Oxfords. We actually had civilian W/T operators in them. In really bad weather they proved their work by getting useful 'fixes' for us. The civilian engineers were also very efficient, we had an excellent serviceability record. We also had an air traffic school and DH Dominies to give them air experience. (The Dominie was the service version of the Rapide.) The Dominie had one marvellous advantage for an instructor, there was only one seat up front! So no dual and a marvellous view ahead. They weren't the easiest aeroplanes to handle on touchdown, and had to be treated with respect.

The winter of 1941–42 was not noted for its good weather. The visibility on the 31st December was 200 yards and 50 feet cloud base; on the 7th January 1942 I carried out four approaches with visibility 800 yards and fog on the ground. That must have been an exaggeration, perhaps it was Scotch mist! It is interesting that I met with most difficult weather whilst flying the Ansons, a much more amenable aircraft for that sort of thing.

At one time my flight commander was an ex-RAF Sergeant Pilot called George Webb; I believe he flew Bristol Bulldogs in Fighter Command in the late 1920s. He was a superb natural pilot and also a calm laid-back natural leader. After the war he worked at AST Hamble and I worked under him again; he became the CFI there. Anyway, on one occasion of thick fog he asked me to find my way to the airfield threshold and confirm that the approach and touchdown area had been cleared of some work in progress there. I managed to do so, but had a hard job to find my way back and report it. This did not deter him one bit; he carried out a successful weather test, but that was one of the few occasions I recall when flying stopped at Watchfield.

We had a satellite 'Beam' at Kelmscott on the upper reaches of the Thames about ten miles north-east of Watchfield – this was in open flat country; the field was not manned at all (in those days many training units had unmanned satellite fields in open country for forced landings etc.) and it was, I suppose, about 800–1,000 yards long. We had a course of Imperial Airways pilots at one time and we staggered them by doing night touch-and-goes on this unlit field.

I had a nostalgic flight on the 17th July 1942. I flew to Worthy Down, north of Winchester, en route to Eastleigh. This was protected by a balloon barrage (it was a Spitfire factory) and one had to land at Worthy Down and phone through a request for them to be hauled down! My old original flying instructor, now Commander Eckersley-Maslin RN, was there and wanted to get to Luton, so we flew together again, the first time for four years, in my Oxford AT781. I dropped him off at Luton and we met once more the following year when he was Captain of RN Air Station at Stretton and used a Hornet Moth (as 'Admiral's Barge,' as they said in the Navy). I look back on that with considerable nostalgia, especially as we never met up again.

On the 27th July 1942 nemesis intervened. I had already done over 83 hours that month (of course flight time limitations were not heard of, in any case there *was* a war on!) and in Oxford AT785 with one pupil under a canvas hood and a second watching seated on the main spar between the two seats, I nodded off from sheer exhaustion on a blind approach. The aircraft hit the middle of the airfield and went over onto its back. The two pupils were fortunately only bruised. The first words I heard as I came to were "Lend me a hacksaw," from the engineer cutting me out of the wreckage.

I spent two weeks in the RAF Hospital at Wroughton, not far away, and two weeks' sick leave at home, and resumed work on the 29th August. There were no particular criticisms at the enquiry; I had been up the night before as duty officer coping with a false air raid alarm, but after all, we *were* at war, and life went on.

The biggest worry for me was the effect on my wife, who was six months' pregnant with our first-born. But all was well, she was very staunch, and Trevor, bless him, has turned out to be a very successful veterinary surgeon. We lived out in a little two-up and one-down cottage in Faringdon, and I had acquired a push-bike with three-speed gear, so I was mobile. When the 'call' came we had to hire a taxi in the middle of the night for a not very romantic moonlight ride to the Radcliffe Hospital at Oxford (17 miles away) where he was born. So romantic after all!

I had been promoted to Flight Lieutenant that summer and made a flight commander, and in December was promoted again to Acting Squadron Leader on posting to command No. 1534 BAT (Beam Approach Training) Flight at No. 11 AFU (Advanced Flying Unit) at RAF Station Shawbury, near Shrewsbury. BAT Flights were small units with about eight Oxfords for training in beam approach at Training and Bomber Command airfields. I had about eight instructors, a Sergeant fitter and rigger, several airmen fitters, riggers and radio mechanics and a marvellous Corporal Administrator who took all the admin burdens off my back (and taught me a thing or two about that side of life!). It was a wonderful family; we were called a 'Lodger Unit' and the CO and staff of the AFU didn't really know how we fitted in to their way of life. To be tolerated I had to exert tact and diplomacy, but it all worked out, especially at one period in mid-winter when we had atrocious weather and for one month my six serviceable Oxfords did more flying than the rest of the station's units.

Shawbury had quite a large Maintenance Unit as well as the AFU and I made friends with their test pilots and got passenger rides in a Beaufighter and Mosquito. Our radio beam was, unfortunately, aligned on the north–south runway on a heading of 012°, so we did not often get an opportunity to land off our approaches. I made a point of taking the Station Commander, Group Captain Divers, on a familiarisation flight and he realised the value of our work, and Air Traffic Control were excellent in allowing us approaches when the other runways were in use. Modern air traffic controllers would have had heart attacks!

I had a great team of instructors, and remember saying to a New Zealand Flight Sergeant pilot at a training session: "Stop wool-gathering, Groves."

"I'm sorry, Sir," he replied, "I was a sheep farmer before I joined up."

CO shuts up!

I had a personal visit from a boffin who was a personal friend of both my wife and myself from TRE (Telecommunication Research Establishment), which had taken over my old school, Malvern. He was engaged in developing advanced blind landing radar, and came up to look at our work. I clearly recall him telling me that they could easily develop a blind (automatic) landing system, but pilots would not trust it until the next generation. How accurate was his prophecy! What they did develop was called GCA (Ground Controlled Approach) which was vastly improved from beam approach, and was literally taken over by the Americans and shares the basis of modern automatic approaches and landings with ILS (Instrument Landing System).

I greatly enjoyed my time at Shawbury. Being my own boss was heady enjoyment. Everybody was friendly and co-operative. I found a very nice bed-sit and use of kitchen with a lovely family at Wem, about three miles from the airfield, and in 1942 I bought in Shrewsbury my first car, a 1934 Standard 9 saloon, registration number UJ 3080, for £40 with 28,912 miles on the clock. I kept it for four years (scrounging extra petrol for it over and above the ration was a work of art!) and sold it for £120!

Eventually all good things come to an end and I left Shawbury in mid-March 1944 for a posting onto operations in Bomber Command, at last! I had, of course, to relinquish my rank of Acting Squadron Leader and revert to Flight Lieutenant, but I just removed the thin ring between the two thicker ones of a Flight Lieutenant and became one of the rare breed of demoted Squadron Leaders evident from the wide spacing of their Flight Lieutenant rings. I now had a total of 2,600 hours.

## CHAPTER 5
# PATHFINDING
## BOMBER COMMAND 1944-1945

Well, it had come, a posting to Bomber Command, and I was a bit mystified at having to go to No. 11 OTU (Operational Training Unit) on Wellingtons, at RAF Westcott near Aylesbury. After a week of ground school I went to the satellite airfield at Oakley (later the scene of the notorious great train robbery) and converted to the 'Wimpy' day and night to a total of 17 hours and 5 minutes.

I found it interesting, after all it was another new type, but it appeared that it was the *hors d'oeuvre* to the main meal, conversion to Mosquitos in No. 8 Group, Air Vice-Marshal Bennett's Pathfinder Force (see Appendix 6). My morale began to recover, but first I was due a couple of nights, 25th & 26th April, at RAF Little Horwood for a session in the decompression chamber. I was sent up (with an attendant) to 37,000 feet, and told not to wear my oxygen mask. On the way up I was asked to write my name, rank and number (as we reached 20,000 feet). I could not control the pencil and felt ludicrous at my inability. I was rational at 20,000 feet but passed out at 26,000. My mask was then put on and I gradually became clearer in my mind and was able to write alternate odd numbers from 100 downwards (but with one lapse). A cautionary tale if ever there was one. I kept this effort in the appropriate page of my log book and a copy is attached (in Appendix 7) which shows it all. I was in that thing for four hours altogether!

Whilst I was at Westcott I read in *"The Telegraph"* that I had been awarded the AFC. To this day I don't know why, as I never saw a citation and it was sent to me in the post – the poor King was much too busy to dish them out!

At last, towards the end of May, I reported to No. 1655 MTU (Mosquito Training Unit) at RAF Warboys in Huntingdonshire, and went solo after 2 hours 25 minutes dual. We also did quite a lot of training in Oxfords, paired up with our navigators and finished the course on the 4th July. I had 4 hours 20 minutes day dual and 30 minutes night dual, 27 hours 40 minutes day solo and 9 hours 30 minutes night solo. Altogether the course total was 94 hours (the rest of the time was on Oxfords). My navigator was one Frank Halpin who had already done a tour on Wellingtons. I was glad to have him and his previous operational experience, but I know I frightened him more than once in the days to come.

We had heard a lot about the Mosquito. Aircraft get reputations from crew-room gossip, but I never heard anything but praise for the "Mossie." it lived up to its reputation and was a superb aircraft for all its different (and difficult) operational roles in which it was used. (The Oxford was a much more difficult aircraft to fly, in my humble opinion.) It was of necessity cramped, but that had advantages for co-operation with one's navigator. It was not easy to get in and out (I was glad I was thin!) but it handled like a dream. I have never heard a bad word spoken about it. Of course, fully bombed-up with maximum fuel (4,000 lb bomb and extra wing fuel tanks) it was a bit of a handful to cope with on take-off and initial climb, and when the 4,000 lb bomb was released the "Mossie" certainly took on a new lease of life!

At extreme altitude there was little, if anything, in reserve to achieve the required performance, but then everything was pushed to (and sometimes beyond) its limits in wartime, a situation that rarely occurred in peacetime flying.

So, operational at last, a posting to No. 105 (PFF) Squadron at Bourn, about 10 miles west of Cambridge, but frustration – an immediate detachment to No. 692 Squadron at Graveley for basic bombing before graduating to the 'Oboe' Pathfinder Mark IXs and Mark XVIs of 105. Frank and I were only a week at Graveley and our first operation was at night to Berlin on 10th July. The squadron used Mark XVIs with the extended (or should I say pregnant distended!) bomb bay in order to carry the 4,000 lb blockbuster bomb. The previous day we had a 50-minute familiarisation flight and on the day itself a 40-minute night-flying test before the actual operation. One is always at one's worst vulnerability on one's first op. We got there, dropped our bomb (what a difference to performance that made!) and got back, not incident-free however. Frank got a bit airsick, and when we made an approach to an airfield, I realised at the last minute that it wasn't Graveley, so I overshot and switched on Graveley's beam approach; we did get back after 4 hours 45 minutes and the refuellers told me that there were only 17 gallons of fuel left in the tanks, i.e. about $8^1/_2$ minutes flying! By such narrow margins do we survive. The squadron CO, Wing Commander Watts, went missing on that raid.

On the night of the 14th July we did our second operation to Hanover. This took 3 hours 40 minutes and passed without incident. After a lie-in we went back to Bourn the next day.

No. 105 Squadron, together with its twin, 109, at Little Staughton, were the two Mosquito Pathfinder squadrons operating under the command of Air Vice-Marshal Donald Bennett, using the newly-developed radar system code-named 'Oboe' in No. 8 Group Bomber Command. AVM Bennett was a forceful and dramatic character of immense drive and talent. He was greatly respected in the group and there was nothing anybody could do better than he could as far as flying was concerned.

'Oboe' was a very accurate radar aid, quite difficult to operate successfully. Probably a third of my raids were aborted because of various difficulties. If the markers could not be accurately dropped they were brought back, and, if dropped, when you got back for a debriefing you were told by the debriefing officer what your bombing or marking error was; this would have been phoned through from one of the ground stations (of which there were three, one on the East Coast and two in Kent).

The signals involved were made in response to a transmitter from the aircraft's 'Oboe' equipment, and the bombing run was, of course, curved as it was on a radius from the ground station. So throughout the bombing or marking run the heading was imperceptibly changing. The navigator got out of his seat and lay on the floor listening to position reports during the run-in and released the bombs or markers when given the appropriate signal. No release signal on a pathfinder marking run would be given if the ground station was not satisfied by any of the necessary criteria – mostly depending on the steadiness and accuracy of the final five or so minutes of the run-in. Being on a line of sight, the longer the range the higher one had to go, so the range was limited to as far as the Rühr in Western Germany until after the invasion, when the ground stations were moved into Europe. The maximum altitude we could attain, 'bombed up,' was about 36,000 feet.

Weather of course was irrelevant to us – if it was too bad for ground markers, sometimes sky markers were used, or if too bad for the main force to operate, we could take bombs instead of markers and do a bit of damage 'on the side,' so to speak. We had a ground trainer, so that we could practise. Although we were vulnerable to fighters, especially on daylight raids, we were seldom molested. I never saw a German aircraft all the time I operated and only very occasionally suffered flak damage. I had two cases of engine failure, but with one engine feathered (turning the airscrew blades into minimum-drag position to stop further rotation that might increase engine damage or fire risk) the dear old "Mossie" behaved rather like an underpowered single-engined aircraft, but with overshoot problems from 200 feet or below.

On my second need to feather, which was in my favourite aircraft (a Mark IX LR507 coded 'F'), I was at somewhat over 25,000 feet over the North Sea (about half way) when during an instrument scan I saw the port engine temperature rising rapidly, so I immediately stopped the engine by feathering it and turned back for home. On the way back, for some unaccountable reason the propeller occasionally turned over a rev or two. I did not jettison the markers, they were not a weight problem (had it been a 4,000 lb bomb that would have gone at once!), but 'F' was a Mark IX which could not take them (and in any case markers did not weigh as heavily as bombs). It was the more recent Mark XVI that had the pregnant belly for the 4,000 lb 'cookie' as we called it.

Anyway, when we got back to Bourn and I turned off the runway after landing a Flight Sergeant fitter called up to me and I opened the window and said to him:

"Although I feathered the propeller, occasionally it would turn over a rev or two – why was that?"

He put his finger on an airscrew blade and moved it easily: all the compression had gone.

It was a very different situation if an engine failed in a Mark XVI carrying a 'cookie.' It happened one night to poor Sergeants Whipp and Burtenshaw shortly after take-off and they didn't have an earthly.

I have been asked: "What was it like?"

Well, I suppose everyone is different, but it was a responsible job that was taken very seriously indeed. We often operated in pairs, in loose formation, so that if the leader's 'Oboe' failed, the follower could take over – this was applicable to daylight operations. When notified you were on for an op you would do an aircraft flight test and when gathered in the operations room for the briefing you would be locked in and get a full briefing on weather, target (and its relative importance in the war effort), height to fly, time on target and details of any enemy counter-measures, if known. Whilst the navigators got on with working out the flight plan quite a few of the pilots played bridge (I honed my bidding skills at Bourn!). Pilots were also given a route card with the courses and times, so that in the event of a navigator being lost, the pilot had basic information how to get back.

We were driven out to our aircraft in dispersal, checked it over, got in and started up. Navigators had great responsibility in working to split-second timing throughout the flight. Take-off was, perhaps, the first critical situation to be got over, especially if one was in a Mark XVI with a 'cookie' and at night. Once safely airborne and climbing up to operational altitude, navigators had to work hard to achieve the end result of getting the pilot to the right place at the right time to receive the signal from the ground station to begin his run up to the target.

When the aircraft's call sign was received the 'Oboe' was switched on and the navigator got down on the floor to receive the signals giving the positions along the line of the 'beam' and to operate the bomb release if and when this was given. When using target indicators this would not be given unless the final few minutes of the run-in achieved the required degree of accuracy. The pilot concentrated hard on making a steady run along the beam which was very narrow indeed and as already mentioned was curved – the longer the range the slower the rate of change of heading and the higher one had to go to receive it. About three minutes before release the pilot opened the bomb doors and then had almost always to open up to full power to overcome the extra drag. Probably all windows except the clear vision panels ahead were iced up, so it was concentration on instruments.

After the markers were released a further short period of flying steadily and accurately was required whilst cameras recorded the results. We were generally too high to be bothered much by flak (anti-aircraft fire), though occasional minor damage was sustained. One did not consider the threat of night-fighters, you probably would not have seen one attacking you. Fortunately the war was over before the German jet fighters were numerous enough to threaten us. On return to base we parked our aircraft in its dispersal and were taken back to the operations room for debriefing, and they already had our results phoned through from the ground stations.

It was impressive to be told what our bombing and marking errors were. Anything over 100 yards was considered third-rate and if we were badly inaccurate we would not be given a release signal if markers were being carried.

We were given a small ration of chocolate before departure and a bacon-and-egg meal on return. The present generation might well say: "So what's so wonderful about a bacon-and-egg meal?" A short dissertation on wartime austerity and rationing is perhaps appropriate here.

Shortly after 1939 food, petrol and clothing were severely rationed, and cooking fats virtually disappeared. Fish and chips was a popular prewar food and the enormous growth of the present fish and chip mentality has, in my opinion, been caused by wartime deprivation. I still get a twinge of conscience if I find any butter left on my plate after a meal and instinctively go easy on it!

Petrol was also a problem; it was severely rationed (and did not come off ration until 1950) and I went much more deeply into my car's fuel consumption than that of the aircraft I flew. Every car I've ever had has had fuel consumption checks, though eventually I got fed up converting litres to gallons, not all that long ago! When I had refuelling problems with the car it was quite an art to coax a garage owner to give three gallons for a two-gallon coupon, and not by any means always successful.

I have already mentioned that there were no signposts or place names, so navigating had to be by the excellent quarter-inch to one mile flying maps we used at that time. One tremendous advantage was the shortage of traffic – cars were few and far between and driving through rather than round London was no problem. I even navigated my car out of London on one occasion by using the sun (but it wasn't very successful!).

The met office at Bourn did not often observe the sun either. I remember once coming back from a night operation; it was daylight when we landed, and walking past the met office for our debriefing I noticed a chink of light coming through a badly blacked-out window. I rapped on it and yelled "Black Out!" and the chink was hurriedly covered up: the met men didn't know it was daylight!

We were not supposed to live out on operations, but a few of us had our wives in Cambridge or nearby and spent as much off-duty time with them as we could. Sometimes I would call up Jean and tell her that I was due for "bacon and eggs," which warned her not to expect me.

Being a wartime-built airfield the conditions at Bourn were rather primitive (in stark contrast to the prewar airfield refinements of, for example, South Cerney). We lived in huts in quite spartan and dispersed conditions, and shared a WAAF batwoman – one per hut, I think, there were four of five small rooms per hut. The mess was also quite unrefined, and offices, flights and sick quarters all very dispersed. The squadron personnel, especially the aircrew, were a splendid and highly-motivated lot, with political affiliations ranging from infra-red to ultra-violet; this became evident at the end of the war when the General Election was called. Speaking from rather dim memory now (no log book entries for verification!) one of us was once the editor of the *"Daily Worker"* – very pro-Stalin. One of our best navigators became a monk after the war.

These differences and attitudes were, of course, completely suppressed until after VE-Day. I don't recall wild parties or pub-crawls or anything like that. Perhaps the contrast in our work to that of Fighter Command moulded our characters in a slightly different way and of course I can only quote experience from this one squadron.

Coinciding with von Runstedt's winter offensive in the Ardennes I had to operate on both Christmas Eve and Boxing Day 1944. Both stuck in my mind, as there was a stable anti-cyclone prevalent, and on the 24th December I took off from Bourn in thick fog which was still there on return. Most of East Anglia was clear but I was prepared to land at Bourn using their beam approach; however I was forbidden to try and told to divert to Graveley which was operating FIDO (Fog Intensive Dispersal Of!) but my 'beam' set went unserviceable and a localised crosswind blew so much smoke across the runway that the airfield was totally obscured at 200 feet. So I had to abort and find a fog-free airfield elsewhere, which I did, at a place called Wratting Common, south-south-east of Cambridge. We landed, arranged for a guard on the aircraft (being 'Oboe'-equipped it was 'classified') and got a lift to the market square at Cambridge, where Frank and I, embarrassed with all our parachutes and other clobber, had to wait for a pick-up truck from Bourn. We were one of the few who did get back and I was able to spend Christmas Day in Cambridge with my wife and baby son who were staying with relations she had there.

On Boxing Day we went out again to mark a target at St. Vith in the Ardennes and when we returned on this occasion East Anglia was crystal clear, completely calm but with thick radiation fog again some 20 miles or so inland: an incredible sight. There was a great black towering cloud from the Graveley FIDO rising up into the cloudless upper sky. This time the 'beam' worked and it was fantastically surreal coming down onto the runway with smoke and flames on each side and the roar of the burners audible over the sound of the engines. It must have cost a king's ransom to burn all that fuel for all that time. There were several other fields equipped with FIDO but they were too expensive to be viable and were not used after the war.

My longest operation was a 'daylight' to Berchesgarten on the 25th April 1945 (my penultimate one also), to go and bomb Hitler. Actually he was not there and there were insurmountable reasons for technical failure: firstly, mountains screened the 'Oboe' transmitters and, secondly, we were at extreme range. It took 4 hours 55 minutes and it was a clear cloudless day. Thankfully the Luftwaffe had been virtually eliminated by then and there was no opposition.

My shortest operation was a 'daylight' on Calais on the 25th September 1944 which took only 1 hour 55 minutes. On the 1st September 1944 I got back my old rank of Squadron Leader, but had to relinquish it again on 4th August 1945 when I left the squadron. After VE-Day we continued flying (the war with Japan not yet being over) and carried out some "Cook's Tours" when we took ground crews on flights over Germany to show them the ghastly devastation.

My navigator, Frank Halpin, left the squadron in late April and contested Acton East as a Liberal in the General Election (he was in reality Labour but not being a paid-up member they would not sponsor him), but he lost his deposit and we lost touch with each other.

For the rest of my stay I had various – all excellent – navigators, most of all a charming Belgian called Jean Delori.

One final episode that was most impressive concerned the mercy missions, a brief campaign to feed the starving Dutch by air drops of food. From the 2nd May 1945 right up to VE-Day on the 8th May I did four of these, marking dropping zones for the heavies on airfields and racecourses. On the 8th May, the last, we came down to ground level, and it was so moving a scene watching the hungry but jubilant Dutch swarming into the dropping zone and waving like mad.

I finally left the Squadron on the 7th August and once again reverted to the rank of Flight Lieutenant. But there was one last final *denouement*: on the 10th September I flew up with my instructor from Elmdon, where I was doing a refresher course on Tiger Moths, to Upwood where No. 105 had relocated and I flew him in "Mossie" Mark XVI PF442 on a "Cook's Tour" over Walcheren, Wesel, Rühr, Hanover, Bremen and Osnabrück and back in 4 hours 45 minutes.

In my log book I wrote: "Shall I ever fly a 'Mossie' again?" Not so very long ago I added the word "No!" to that entry.

End of an era. 39 daylight, 37 night operations, four mercy missions, total 80.

CHAPTER 6
# POST-WAR RAF SERVICE
## INSTRUCTING AGAIN 1945-1947

When it became obvious to us all that the war in Europe would not last much longer, many of us turned our thoughts to what we would (or could) do as civilians. Our AOC, AVM Donald Bennett, issued some useful guidelines for those who wanted to fly as a civilian career (and from time to time I had studied some of the required subjects for the 'B' or commercial licence, including nav and met).

He himself left the service and founded British South American Airways, and a few from our squadron joined that firm, and eventually as it merged with BOAC became employed by that organisation. I had no desire to go on long-haul, and decided to go back to instructing; half the pay, twice the pleasure! In any case we had a five-year-old son and wanted more! A life as a professional civil flying instructor appealed to me, and I began to study seriously for the 'B' licence. The RAF conveniently sent me to No. 14 EFTS (Elementary Flying Training School) at Elmdon, Birmingham. The course lasted a month, August–September 1945, and there I did my first night flying in a single-engined aircraft – the good old Tiger Moth, of course.

From there I was posted to No. 10 (Elementary) Flying Instructors School at Woodley near Reading. My wife and son meanwhile remained in the home we had in Cambridge (it was a requisitioned council house) as I hoped to get back there. On the 3rd October I went to the Air Ministry in London to take the exam for the 'B' licence. That passed off all right.

One needed an aircraft type endorsed on the licence and I had opted for the Mosquito. However it was not a practical choice when I discussed it, so I changed to the Tiger Moth and after a log book scrutiny this was done. Normally a written technical exam and a brief flight test was required for a type endorsement but that was waived in this case.

There was one further problem, a requirement for a night cross-country landing at an airfield different from that of departure. Now I had never done a night cross-country with an 'away' landing and I discussed this problem with one of the examiners. I did then mention the occasion in 1940 during night dual circuits with a pupil from Bibury when I 'lost' our glim lamp flarepath in the thick haze and 'found' Windrush and landed there, not realising where I was until I saw I was among Ansons instead of Oxfords! But a benevolent official allowed that for the issue of the licence. In those days civil servants were both civil and human!

I enjoyed my course at Woodley; it lasted until the 23rd November and took 74$^1$/$_2$ hours (of which 7 hours 55 minutes was at night); 10 hours 25 minutes were on the Magister, the rest on the Tiger Moths.

The CO, Wing Commander Moir AFC, was in actuality Miles' manager, and I flew with him in the "Maggie"; as a salesman for Miles he made a point of praising the aircraft, and in particular for its spin-recovery qualities (prewar there had been fatal accidents through difficulty in recovery and it had been suitably and efficiently modified to rectify the fault).

The story going round Woodley at the time was that he was quoted as saying: "All this fuss about difficulty in spin recovery in the Magister is rubbish, you can do precision spin recoveries as I will demonstrate. Here we are at 3,000 feet facing Reading. I will do three turns and recover on Reading. Here we go – Reading one, Reading two, Reading three – recover – Reading four – oh! b*****, Basingstoke!"

On the 3rd December 1945 I reported to No. 22 EFTS at Cambridge: so far, so good. We trained courses of gunners as Army Air Observation Post pilots and Sergeants as Glider Tug Pilots, so as well as Tiger Moths we had Auster IIIs and later the Lycoming-engined Auster V. I also had a few rubber-assisted take-offs in Kirby Cadet gliders used to give air experience to cadets of the Air Training Corps. We often started early in the morning, and one of my pupils penned an appropriate cartoon (see Appendix 8).

The 6th February 1946 was a traumatic day: 17 Tiger Moths at the three dispersals were damaged by a severe gale that sprung up unexpectedly, and on the 19th February, just after landing, I turned out of wind on a slight slope, and my Tiger was blown over onto its back by a sudden unexpected line squall. Hanging upside down helplessly on the shoulder straps was a horrible and humiliating feeling, both for me and my pupil, one Sergeant Griffiths. Anyway, the engine was stopped and the fire tender quickly came out and extricated us both safely!

One student I well remember was Major Kennedy, who eventually went on to command the Army Air Training School at Middle Wallop, from where he flew down to Hamble for a reunion and flight together in the latest version of the Auster.

On the 9th May 1946 I flew with student Captain Molyneux-Berry on a cross-country to Sywell and was greeted on my return by the news of the birth of our second son, Clive. I was hugely chuffed, first born Oxford, second Cambridge – would they ever quarrel over the boat race? No, they didn't ever!

In July 1946 I had another dose of nostalgia. I was detached for a week for a 'Beam' course at Watchfield. I felt it was totally unnecessary: there were hundreds of pilots with no experience of it, why send me back there!? Nevertheless I enjoyed it, though my instructor (who probably had a tenth of my experience on it) was horrified when I suggested we should try some blind landings.

One amusing non-flying incident took place at this time. I took an unofficial trip into town in my old Standard 9 one morning, to be greeted on my return to dispersal by rather worried ground engineers. They had, unbeknown to me, removed my front number plate to repaint it, as it was in such a bad state of repair. Technically I had committed an offence by going on public roads without it and they were concerned. So they bolted it back on and I noticed that it was JJ 3080 when it should have been UJ 3080! Had they put it back without my knowing, goodness knows how long it would have been before it was discovered. So all was well and it (the 'J') got suitably enlarged to a 'U.' It shows how bad a state it was in, though. The dear old car had done me proud for 3,000 miles and was replaced after 6 years by an Austin 10, more suitable for a growing family.

# CHAPTER 7
# CIVVY STREET
## RAFVR/CIVIL 1947-1949

And so, after seven years in the Service, I was demobilised in May 1947, but retained in the RAF Volunteer Reserve. I had to go to Manchester, I think it was, and spend one night being issued with civilian clothes, ration books, etc. It had been a very cold winter and so was the next. Rationing was as severe as in wartime and an enormous amount of reconstruction was in hand. For people living in the UK in these early postwar years life was a hard slog. In March 1947 one example was the severe flooding all along the Bedford levels and at Earith in East Anglia. I flew as passenger up front in a DC-3 (G-AGIP) piloted by Marshall's CFI, Les Worsdell, to make a survey; it was an amazing spectacle, it stretched for miles and miles.

Worsdell was now my boss. Arthur Marshall (now Sir Arthur) interviewed me before my demob and gave me a job as an RAFVR/Civilian Instructor. With my growing family it was a comfort to be demobbed with a job to go to, especially as it did not involve a move. I lived in a requisitioned council house in Milton Road – a nice little detached three-bedroom house with off-street parking and a garden. I recall being allocated (everything was rationed) a gas-operated refrigerator, an unheard-of luxury in those days! The neighbours were friendly and tolerant and did not resent our presence. In July 1948 our third son James arrived, but we had to wait for our move to Southampton before our daughter Rosemary came to complete the family. Towards the end of our final months at Cambridge we were transferred to a newly-built council house, not nearly so nice, and we were not there long before we moved away.

My life as a RAFVR/Civilian Instructor was varied and pleasant, with a salary about the same as I had been getting in the RAF. Under Les Worsdell there was a very good team of instructors. As well as both service and civil Tiger Moths we flew (as civilians) Austers, a Proctor, a Gemini and DH Rapides – the latter I had flown at Watchfield six years earlier. But it nearly broke my heart that I was not allowed to test the Mosquitos that were being turned out by the Maintenance Unit there.

We ran a very good service to race meetings for the trainers, owners and jockeys from nearby Newmarket, sometimes landing on the racecourses themselves. We used the Rapides, occasionally a Gemini, Proctor or sometimes even the Auster for an individual charter. Weather was always a concern, and so as not to let them down each pilot was given the names and phone numbers of his next day's passengers and it was his responsibility to check the weather in time to tell his clients, if necessary, to go by alternative transport if we couldn't guarantee to get them there. Sometimes an individual jockey would charter the Auster for some race meeting or other. On the Rapides we carried a wireless operator but there was no R/T, nor such luxuries as precision blind approaches to most of our destinations, often no civil air traffic control either!

I recall one charter to York races in bad weather, and I was flying under low cloud over the plain of Lincolnshire, following the railway. A worried jockey poked his head into the cockpit and asked: "Are we going to get there?"

I pointed down to the railway and said: "Do you see that train down there? It's the 7.50 to York and I am following it!"

Arthur Marshall, our dynamic boss, was an excellent pilot in his own right. Once I had to take a Rapide down to Old Sarum and bring him and his wife back to Cambridge. He was so frantically busy all the time that he hardly ever had time to fly himself, so I said to him: "Why don't you fly us back, Sir?", which he did.

Now the Rapide was not a forgiving aeroplane if not landed very carefully, but I needn't have worried: he made one of those perfect three-point merges with the ground, the hallmark of a good pilot. He is still a hale and hearty nonagenarian at the time of writing.

I had the 'privilege' of sending his son Michael on his first solo, in a Tiger, on the 31st March 1948, fairly early in the morning. He received some further instruction and some solo, in the same day, for obtaining his 'A' licence and by the end of the day he had qualified for the licence. A splendid effort on his part (and possibly a record?). Anyway, I believe he is now Lord Lieutenant of Cambridgeshire and probably hasn't the time to fly much, but I bet he still remembers that day!

I led a curious sort of hybrid life at Marshall's, as I was basically employed as an instructor on the RAFVR school which operated service Tiger Moths, but the civilian side was so varied and interested that I was delighted that the firm used me on that side as much as they did. I did several quite long flights in an Auster Autocrat G-AJUH to Luxembourg, and the Proctor and Gemini lent variety, which to me was the spice of life – not to mention, of course, the Rapides that they operated.

I recall getting into trouble, quite rightly, bringing back a party of racegoers from Hereford one winter's night in bad weather, when I was advised not to attempt the flight. However, urged by my passengers, I decided to have a go and if necessary divert to Oakington nearby. I found Cambridge and had to orbit whilst a flare path was laid. The passengers were delighted and I think that because of that the CFI did not take me to task as much as he was justified. It was not really a good professional decision on my part. War- and peace-time flying have different parameters.

I think I've already mentioned it, but it is worth repeating that the Rapide/Dominie had one marvellous quality, especially for an instructor, in that there was only one seat and one set of controls up front: it was all and undisputedly *all* yours!

I twice had charters to Heathrow in the Rapides, but we had no R/T, only a W/T operator, and getting in and out was tricky, but we coped – quite impossible nowadays!

Another memorable flight I had, which was at night, was on the 27th & 28th March 1948. I was last on duty in the office that evening when a rather distressed young woman with a companion came in and wanted to get to Prestwick in Scotland. We phoned her father and verified that he would pay COD, so to speak, and confirmed that the airfield would stay open. So we had a long night haul, getting there about midnight. We collected the fare from a relieved father, and my W/T operator and I found a bed each for the rest of the night. When the airfield re-opened the next morning we flew back, arriving at Cambridge about midday, and had the rest of that day off!

The 27th of October 1947 was a red letter day for our CFI Les Worsdell, his deputy Gordon Hubbard and for me. Every so often the 'trappers' as they were called (the visiting flight of the Central Flying School), who travelled around testing flying instructors and their pupils, gave us a test, and as a result we were upgraded to CFS category A1, the top grade for instructors, so well worth the hassle. Outside the flying profession it is perhaps not generally known that pilots have frequent tests – competency tests, type rating tests, instructor renewal tests, instrument rating tests, medical tests – you name it, a pilot has to prove it. It's not popular, but particularly for instructors, who give tests to others, it is a good thing as when we sit in the examiner's seat ourselves we know how those we test are feeling, and have the experience to make a certain amount of allowance for 'testitis'!

In 1948 a young 18-year-old, Wendy Sabberton, joined the staff in the flight office and had a return trip in the back of Autocrat G-AGXX to Stradishall, where she organised joyrides for Empire Air Day. She also 'baby sat' for Jean and myself and she had a ride with me in a Tiger on an air test in August 1949. When we left Cambridge contact was temporarily lost, but she married and came to live in Southampton (where we then lived) and the intermittent relationship continued. She then learned to fly at Eastleigh and played a not insignificant part in getting me back into flying in the 1970s – but of that more later.

On the 12th March 1948 I had a race charter to Blackpool. Whilst there waiting to bring the passengers back I saw my very first Chipmunk on the tarmac, G-AKCS, recently imported from Canada, and possibly the first one in the UK. I could not resist the temptation to fly it, and had a quick dual check and a quick solo circuit. Little did I realise then how many hours I would clock up on that utterly delightful type.

I had an interesting charter in Autocrat G-AJUH to Cardiff on the 22nd June 1949. It was a hazy day with no wind and I had to keep fairly low to maintain sight of the ground. I could not fathom why I kept wandering off track: it became very worrying and I had to sweat a bit to get the passenger to his destination. When we got out and walked into Air Traffic Control to report, I noticed that his left leg was very stiff and he limped badly.

"Have you got an artificial leg?" I asked him.

"Yes," he replied, "why do you ask?"

I felt so relieved at a rational explanation for my haphazard wanderings and I explained to him that the compass, being on the floor between the two front seats, had been affected by his magnetism. (The weather improved for the return, and in any case getting home is easier!)

On one occasion, at least, weather *did* stop me getting home. I had the unenviable job of towing a Kranich sailplane (owned by the Cambridge University Gliding Club) in Tiger Moth G-AIBN from Cambridge to the Long Mynd gliding centre in Shropshire for the annual camp. There was a very strong headwind and I had to land at Wolverhampton to refuel. We got airborne, but the weather really began to close in and with the high ground of Wenlock Edge ahead I did not relish the safety margin. I took the glider as near as I could to its destination and released it over a suitable field. (It should be appreciated that a towed glider was below its tug to avoid slipstream so it was probably even hairier for them.) The glider was successfully retrieved by Long Mynd. I got back as far as Wolverhampton and spent the night there, and the following day returned home. That was on the 14th & 15th March 1949.

Glider-towing was quite a busy occupation at Marshall's, as the Cambridge University Gliding Club was very active at that time. I had one or two enjoyable flights with them. Marshall's at that time charged 10/– for a tow to 2,000 feet and 5/– per thousand feet thereafter. When the glider was released we hared back to the airfield, dropped the tow-rope, did a quick circuit and landed. It wasn't safe or feasible to drop the rope and land at the same time. I greatly enjoyed the small bit of gliding and soaring I was able to do and would have liked to develop it, but hadn't the time.

The family was increasing – our third son James was born in 1948 – and I had the extra commitment (of which more anon) of running an Air Training Corps squadron. However, just before I left Cambridge for good, I got Jean airborne with me for the first and only time – the day after her birthday, the 9th October 1949. She hated flying, and even later on when flying far afield as a passenger in British Airways she did not enjoy it one bit. But I loved her just as much, perhaps even more!

Having done quite a lot of formation flying in the Service, we also did some on the Reserve School at Cambrdige and I greatly enjoyed it. Worsdell, our CFI, was a pilot of outstanding ability and the success of a good formation does very much depend on having a good leader, which he was. He led several formations of nine aircraft or more, and once, with the minimum of rehearsal, he led two of us, himself leader, Gordon Hubbard (deputy CFI) No. 2 on his right and me No. 3 on his left, in a short display, on one of Cambridge's Air Days on the 16th July 1949, of tied-together formation. This required intense concentration, especially as it was at a public display, but we did it, and would you believe it, the hardest part (to me at any rate) was the taxying!

The *"Cambridge Daily News"* of that date reported the event as follows:

### THEY FLEW TIED TOGETHER

#### R.A.F.V.R. "At Home" Demonstration

*The spectacle of three Tiger Moths tied together, flying in formation was one of the highlights of the "At Home" organised by Cambridge R.A.F.V.R. at Marshall's Airport on Saturday.*

*Three instructors of No. 22 Reserve Flying School, Squadron Leaders L.V. Worsdell, A.W. Farrell and H.G. Hubbard piloted the aircraft concerned. It was one of the most impressive exhibitions of formation flying seen at Cambridge for a long time.*

However the time had come for a change, and in October 1949 we moved down to Southampton to join Air Service Training at Hamble. This meant a salary rise from £600 to £800 p.a., badly needed with a growing family as our third son James had arrived in July 1948. I had just paid a deposit cheque on a house in Cambridge before getting the new job offer confirmed, but I managed to stop the cheque, to the estate agent's great annoyance!

So farewell Cambridge. I enjoyed my years here, the lovely town and river, good friends and a wonderfully interesting and varied flying job, but we did not regret the decision to leave.

Finally, just a word about my involvement with the Air Training Corps during my period at Marshall's. Cambridge had a thriving ATC squadron, No. 104, and Marshall was chairman of the Governing Committee. When the CO retired, Marshall asked me if

I would take over. I did not relish the idea as there was not much time for family life anyway, but I decided I had better go along with it if I wanted to consolidate my career prospects. One of their officers, Flying Officer Don Snazle, ex-RAF navigator and a serving police constable in the Cambridge constabulary, was also interviewed for the job. After our formal interviews by the organising committee we waited together outside while a decision was being reached, and I suggested to Don, and he agreed, that whichever of us was chosen, the other would be happy to serve as adjutant, a post also vacant. He readily agreed and when we were called in before the committee I told them what we had discussed and this went down very well.

In the event Don proved to be a tower of strength as adjutant and I was pleased that he took over as CO when I left after a run of about two years. We had a big squadron, upwards of 50 or so I think, and like all good squadrons it thrived because of the excellent qualities of the cadet NCOs we had. Warrant Officer Bing, the senior NCO, was a firm and fair disciplinarian and I was pleased that he got a flying scholarship from Marshall; I had the pleasure of giving him dual. We also had two very good Sergeants, Gathercole and Tresize.

All our cadets were keen and well-motivated. Apart from drills, parades, ground school and games, they got an annual summer camp at an RAF station, gliding instruction and air experience.

I remember some of them being given an early experience of evasion when, two at a time, some of them were loaded into Marshall's Austers, blindfolded and landed into fields in the Fens north of Cambridge and told to find their way back; all were successful!

We paraded once or twice an evening in our HQ in Rathmore Road and on Sunday mornings in a car park for drill. I must say I wish I had had a bit more personal freedom, this was one of the reasons I looked for work elsewhere. But they were a fine bunch of young men and we also had other excellent officers and civilian instructors. Perhaps, for me anyway, the best bit was the year our annual summer camp was at RAF Thorney Island and I took down one of the Reserve School's Tiger Moths and spent the week giving them air experience.

53

When I went down to Hamble in October 1949 I did a spell on the committee of the Southampton ATC Squadron under chairman Bruce Gilbert, Southampton and Winchester bookseller and ex-RAF Typhoon pilot, but I did not persist for long.

About a year or so ago I was sent from Cambridge a small booklet telling the history of No. 104 (Cambridge) Squadron ATC and I got quite a favourable mention in it. Nice to know after 49 years that one's efforts were appreciated!

## CHAPTER 8

# AIR UNIVERSITY, PART I (1949–1960)
## LIFE AT AIR SERVICE TRAINING, HAMBLE

We moved down from Cambridge in October 1949. I had done a reconnaissance and found a suitable house in Southampton in which to live, and I started work at Air Service Training, Hamble, on the 19th October 1949.

On a family note at this stage, 15 months after our arrival our family was completed by the birth of our beautiful daughter Rosemary. In those days domestic help was reasonably available and off-duty life carried on harmoniously; we moved to a large family house with a nice garden and domestic life was settled and happy.

AST was part of the Hawker Siddeley Group and I already knew many of the personnel there from Watchfield days. They had a diverse fleet of Ansons, Oxfords, two Proctors and one Whitney Straight, two Lycoming-engined Auster Vs and 12 Tiger Moths. In addition the RAF Volunteer Reserve School ran Tiger Moths, and there was a newly-formed Air Navigation School with Avro Ansons. There were also the Maintenance Unit and Southampton University Air Squadron.

So Hamble literally seethed with aircraft movements, and the general lack of incidents, much less accidents, was a tribute to the pilots, pupils and Air Traffic Control – not many aircraft had R/T in those days. In due course the Tiger Moths were replaced by six Chipmunks and two Auster Aiglet trainers. I collected the first Chipmunk, G-AMUC, from the DH factory at Hawarden on the 30th October 1952.

Our students came from all over the world. The worst were the Persians (hopeless!); it's difficult to say who were the best, but the lovely little Burmese stood out. Israelis and Jordanians were good, and I forged a particularly strong friendship with an Indian who went on to have a very distinguished career in Indian and Canadian aviation. He ended up as a high official in ICAO at

Montreal, from where he still travels round the world on trouble-shooting missions – and he still keeps in touch with me!

Memories come flooding back as I browse through my log books: retrieving a lost student (who later became C. in C. of the Saudi Arabian Air Force) in a Tiger Moth from a field in Wiltshire: and going up to Newbury on a night cross-country in a Chipmunk with a Nigerian, taking over and slow-rolling it to topple the artificial horizon to see how he coped with it! Earlier, when we did night cross-countries in Tiger Moths I remember seeing one ahead of me (we were both en route to Christchurch), switching off my navigation lights, opening up the throttle and coming alongside him and flashing my torch at him!

Night-flying in those days was primitive – there was no radio, of course – and back at the airfield there was an old-fashioned flarepath of paraffin flares just as in the earliest days. But we did have an angle of approach indicator to help (amber: too high, green: correct, red: too low).

One final memory of night-flying in Chipmunks is of an ex-Luftwaffe German pilot on a solo flight exercise who missed the airfield and went on westwards. Fortunately by now we did have radio, and as his calls got fainter I took off in another Chipmunk and called him up from the air. I eventually got him to turn round and caught sight of him. I got him back safely – a happy ending.

We had an RAFVR unit at Hamble, operating Chipmunks, and we could combine our annual training with work. I remember one day sending a rather unreliable Iraqi on a solo cross-country to Blandford, getting into an RAF Chipmunk and following out behind him in line astern (he never saw me, naturally!). He went in the general direction of Blandford but never got there. I broke off pursuit in time to get back first and greet him on his return.

"Did you get there all right?" I asked.

"Oh! Yes, Sir," he replied.

Flight time limitations were not known in those early postwar days. On the 25th August 1954 I logged 8 hours and 25 minutes. We started work at 08.30 and it was about midnight when I got home. I found myself squeezing shaving cream on my toothbrush; how accident-prone can you get?

TOP: Red and white Hornet Moth G-ADMM, in which the author took his first flying lessons in 1936.
BOTTOM: BAC Drone G-AEEN, the second type that the author flew solo, on the 1st November 1936.
Photos: author's collection.

TOP: Gladys Batchelor in the all-silver BA Swallow G-AERK, seen before she and Tony Farrell flew to Plymouth on the 24th July 1937. Photo: the author.
BOTTOM: The start of the Plymouth Air Race on the 24th July 1937. Elwell's Taylor Cub is seen getting away, and Alington's Dart Kitten is next in the line. Photo: probably from "Flight," via the author.

TOP: The author in Tipsy S.2 G-AEWJ after his flight on the morning of the 6th June 1937. Photo: author's collection.
BOTTOM: The Tipsy in the afternoon of the same day, after its crash. Photo: the author.

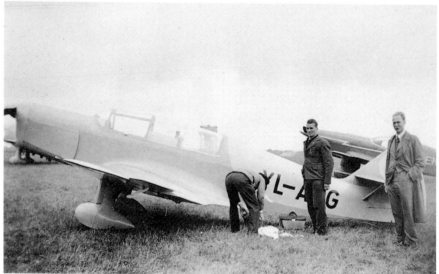

TOP: The author (on L.) works on Henshaw's Mew Gull G-AEXF immediately prior to the Thanet Air Race on the 21st August 1937. Photo: author's collection.

BOTTOM: The unusual Latvian VEF.12 YL-ABG, another participant in the Thanet Air Race. Photo: the author.

TOP: Spartan Arrow G-ABOB, another type flown by the author, on the 31st July 1937.
Photo: the author.
BOTTOM: Henri Mignet and his cabin Pou du Ciel at Ramsgate on the 3rd August 1936. This photo is personally signed on the back by M. Mignet.
Photo: author's collection.

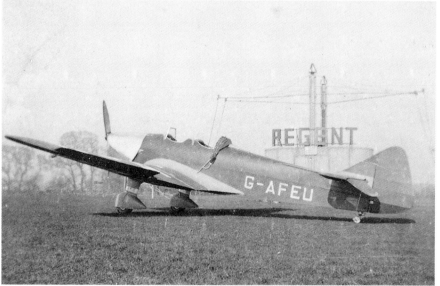

TOP: The Southern Martlet G-AAYX, in which the author soloed on the 3rd July 1938.

BOTTOM: The Magister G-AFEU, in which the author reached 21,000 feet on the 10th April 1938.

Photos: the author.

TOP: Gipsy Moth G-ABBV, another type flown by the author.
BOTTOM: The unique Taylor Cub G-AFFJ with the single-bladed propeller.
Photos: the author.

TOP: The tug "Alerto" alongside the quay at Mindelo St. Vincent, Cape Verde Islands. The Company office is in the right background.
BOTTOM L.: A group (Rawlinson, Smee and the author) going out to a coaling on "Alerto" – note the white suits.
BOTTOM R.: The author, now not so white, pictured after an all-night coaling of the Dutch ship "Leersum." All photos: author's collection.

TOP: The tug brings out a lighter of coal. Photo: the author.
BOTTOM L.: Sacks are filled and hoisted by the ship's derrick. Photo: the author.
BOTTOM R.: "My feet have always troubled me (one reason why I flew all I could!)." Photo: author's collection.

TOP: The sacks are emptied into the ship's bunkers, overseen by a Cabo Verdean policeman. Photo: the author.
BOTTOM: The voyage home on the "Bussum." Here the author is helping Captain Hillen wash his dog, "Wally Simpson." Photo: author's collection.

TOP: Changing the guard at Pembroke College, Cambridge, 1940.
BOTTOM: One Englishman (the author) and three Aussies (Harry Tamblyn,
Ian Esplin and Blondie Nevett) at Pembroke College, February 1940.
Photos: author's collection.

No. 36 Course, No. 3 S.F.T.S., South Cerney. The author is second from the right in the back row. Photo: by courtesy of the Ministry of Defence, © Crown Copyright/MOD.

No. 1 (War) Course, Sept./Oct. 1940, No. 2 C.F.S. Cranwell. The author is third from the right in the second row from the front. Other famous names in light aviation include the prewar instructors Ranald Porteous (extreme left, front row) and Geoffrey Alington (fourth from right, front row).
Photo: by kind permission of the Air Officer Commanding and Commandant, Royal Air Force College Cranwell.

TOP: The author (R) briefs a Polish student, Cpl. Kocjan) prior to night-flying at Bibury in an Oxford on the 23rd October 1941.
BOTTOM: Night-flying sortie in an Oxford at Bibury, 1941. The author is third from the left.
Photos: Central Press via the author.

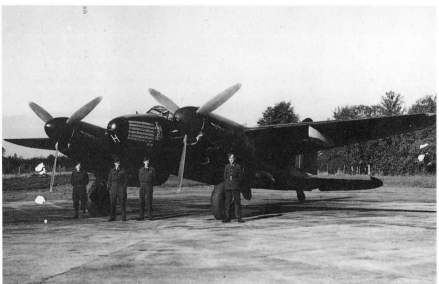

TOP: The author's favourite "Mossie," the Mk. IX LR507 'F' for Freddie, seen at Bourn in 1944. Photo: the author.
BOTTOM: Another 105 Squadron "Mossie," Mk. IX LR504 'H,' again at Bourn during August 1944. Photo: by courtesy of the Ministry of Defence, © Crown Copyright/MOD.

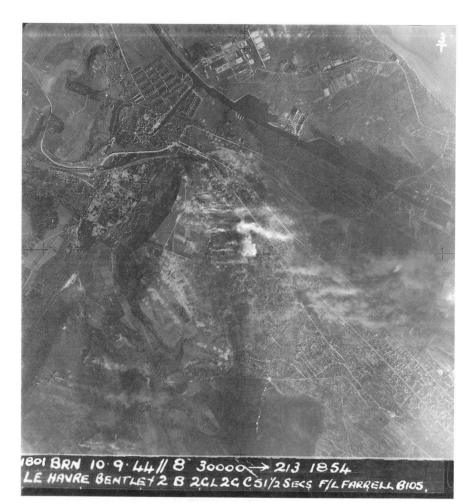

German enclave besieged at Le Havre.
Photo: by courtesy of the Ministry of Defence, © Crown Copyright/MOD.

Fuel storage raid on Dortmund during daylight (bombing error 35 yd).
Photo: by courtesy of the Ministry of Defence, © Crown Copyright/MOD.

TOP: A personal snapshot during formation flying. After VE-Day personal cameras could be used. Photo: the author.

BOTTOM: A mercy mission taking groceries to Holland on VE-Day, the 8th May 1945. L-R: Gordon, Potts, De Lisle, Delori, Lake, S/L Farrell, G/C Somerville (CO), S/L Bishop. Photo: author's collection.

No. 104 (Cambridge) Squadron ATC, 1947.
Photo: by courtesy of the Ministry of Defence, © Crown Copyright/MOD.

TOP: The author leading a parade of No. 104 Squadron (Cambridge) ATC, 1948.
BOTTOM: Arthur (now Sir Arthur) Marshall congratulating ATC Warrant Officer Bing on his flying scholarship, Cambridge 1948. The author is on the left, and a Tiger Moth G-AIBN and a Rapide are seen in the background.
Photos: Cambridge Daily News via the author.

TOP: At the close of a photographic sortie from Hamble on the 19th March 1952 in Tiger Moth G-ALWW. L-R: Russell Adams, CFI Wg. Cdr. Henry Stratton, the author.
BOTTOM: Out on a limb – and a wing! What a photographer will do for a good shot. Russell Adams is the brave man in – or on – G-ALND.
Photos: Cyril Peckham/Hawker-Siddeley via the author.

TOP: Russell Adams' view of the author during the photographic sortie in March 1952. Photo: Russell Adams/Hawker-Siddeley via the author.

BOTTOM: A rare 'prang' at Hamble on the 3rd October 1955, caused possibly by ground resonance. Fortunately there were no injuries. The helicopter was Hiller UH-12B G-AOFK.

Photos: Hawker-Siddeley via the author.

1954: a group of Indonesian students at Air Service Training line up in front of a Dakota IV. This photo was sent to the author in appreciation. Photo: author's collection.

TOP: Hamble's first civil Chipmunk, G-AMUC. The author is in the back seat.
BOTTOM: Ex-Luftwaffe and ex-RAF reunion at Hamble! The author looks happier than his student!
Photos: author's collection.

TOP: The author fields a question from a student in a C.A.T. Apache, April 1960. Photo: author's collection.
BOTTOM: Barry Nicholson in his Grob G-BMGR at Lasham, 1989.
Photo: Barry Nicholson via the author.

Golden Wedding family group at Milford-on-Sea on the 9th August 1991.
Photo: author's collection.

We trained navigators as well as pilots, and one of my most pleasant memories was in April 1951 when I flew Anson G-AHNT from Hamble to Eastleigh (for customs)–Lyons (overnight stop)–Rome (overnight stop)–Malta (day off!)–Sardinia (refuelling stop)–Lyons (overnight stop)–Eastleigh (for customs)–Hamble. Coming back over the Channel the haze was very thick and in spite of three navigators (and the pilot!) I had a helluva job to find Eastleigh. Johnny Plowman was the staff navigator, and the two Burmese trainees were Kyaw and Wiltshire – how he got that name as a Burmese we never knew.

Then two Dakotas were brought in to complete a contract for training a large number of Indonesian pilots; they were splendid young men. I was quite glad I didn't fly the Dakotas myself. Hamble was a very small, awkwardly-shaped grass airfield for such aircraft, and our longest run was about 1,100 metres (1,200 yards) north-south, very much a limit field for Dakotas.

Before the RAFVR changed their Tiger Moths for Chipmunks, we occasionally used to fly with a fellow instructor to practise instrument flight 'under the hood.' I remember doing quite a successful loop under it, and then my colleague Bob Whitehead did so when we changed over.

It was nice to be able to do some aerobatics occasionally, as it wasn't in the commercial flying syllabus. Neither was formation flying, but we had a few opportunities for that when commercial cameramen came to take air-to-air pictures, as in the accompanying photo. This was taken on the 19th March 1952, when the Hawker-Siddeley Group sent down two photographers for publicity purposes. They were Cyril Peckham and Russell Adams, whom I had the pleasure of taking up. They were original and daring in their work, quite unperturbed by the close formation, noise and wind of the Tiger's open cockpit. This was a wonderful opportunity for Henry and me to do some close formation flying, which I liked very much (in fact I'd done it tied together at Cambridge a few years earlier).

There was a happy sequel to this session, as many years later Cyril Peckham retired to the Isle of Wight; as I was still working at Hamble for the College of Air Training, as it was called by then, I flew over to meet him again for a very pleasant reunion.

The Oxfords were used for twin-engined conversion and instrument rating training. This became obligatory, and we all had to undergo annual renewal tests with examiners from the Ministry of Civil Aviation. This was good for us, as it reminded us what it was like to be on the receiving end of a test instead of giving one! Also, instructors had to undergo a renewal test every two years and medicals every six months. I used to go to RAF Thorney Island for mine and I still remember the bottom line on the eyesight card:

A E L O C H T

Later on we had our own resident doctor at Hamble; not so long ago I passed him on our golf course as he was searching for a lost ball, and remarked to my golf partner that "Apart from my wife, that man knows more about my body than anyone else!"

I mentioned earlier that we had some German pilots at Hamble. These were ex-Luftwaffe pilots doing a short refresher course ready for restarting the German state airline Lufthansa, which had not functioned since about 1940. We all got on very well; my pupil was Col. Eduard Neumann, who had flown against the RAF in the Western Desert. We had mutual respect for one another and became good friends.

For a short time we had two Hiller helicopters for training, although I was not in on that act. One had a disastrous prang, luckily without casualties. The two instructors on the Hillers were Len "Tubby" Fieldhouse and Dick Hazlehurst, who took me up on an air test in G-AOFK on the 1st September 1955. He showed me a 'backwards autorotation' to overcome the unlikely situation of an engine failure just after passing the only suitable space for a forced landing. I was scared out of my wits: he dived to keep sufficient speed up for the rotors to keep going, and then went backwards, losing height rapidly, until the space came into view. He then changed quite abruptly to forward and downward flight to make a successful forced landing. Not for me, thank you very much – going backwards with a failed engine indeed!

A flight I did in Oxford G-AITF on the 17th April 1957 got into the *"Southampton Echo,"* as I witnessed a fire breaking out in the New Forest. I radioed Eastleigh with a warning and they alerted the fire services. 1,500 acres were affected and it took eleven hours to extinguish.

Now an amusing incident very much tied up with a foreigner's reluctance to 'lose face.' On the 23rd February 1950 our duty air traffic controller got a phone call from a solo Persian cadet on a cross-country flight in a Tiger Moth. Roughly, the conversation went something like this:

"Please, Sir, I was lost but I have landed and I know where I am. May I come back by myself?"

"Where are you, then?" the controller asked.

"Sir, I am at Uphill Landing."

"No! Stay where you are and we will fetch you."

I took the pupil's instructor to get him back. He had landed at Worthy Down, near Winchester, where there was a large notice cut into the chalk warning 'uphill landing' on a steep uphill part of that airfield. The cunning so-and-so had sneaked off to a public phone box to try and get out of 'loss of face'!

We had an interesting house magazine called *"Astra"* that was issued a couple of times before the take-over. I had a short story and a poem in it; the story won me a £2 prize in a competition. This was in 1950 and featured the demise of the Tiger Moth – how misguided I was! Now with the benefit of hindsight I realise that I had insulted its sacred presence and made a mockery of its staying powers. As a tribute to that wonderful aircraft the story has been reproduced as the final chapter in this book

I would like to end with another tribute, this time to the ground engineers. They were marvellous blokes (one had pulled me out of a crashed Oxford at Watchfield in 1942). Perhaps if I say that about half my total experience was on single-engined aircraft, and that I never once had an engine failure, that is the best way of showing my appreciation.

## CHAPTER 9
# CORPORATE BODIES
### COLLEGE OF AIR TRAINING 1960-1972

Early in 1960 things began to slow down; no large foreign contracts were coming in, the last of any size being the Indonesians, and so we were relieved to learn that a consortium of BOAC and BEA were to take over from the 1st May 1960 to train suitable candidates for their fleets, as the supply of wartime and postwar ex-service pilots was drying up.

So opened at Hamble a completely new prospect of a high-grade specialist training organisation, to train suitable candidates for their fleets, English candidates! And our pay and conditions of service were vastly improved – not only a sizeable salary increase, but fringe benefits such as health insurance, five-day week, more generous leave entitlement and a staff pension scheme: that really was a bonus, there had been nothing like that before. The aircraft were standardised with Chipmunks for basic training and Piper Apaches with airline radio for the second year. (It was a two-year course, one year basic, one year advanced training.) The students did alternate days in ground school and flights.

There was also a liberal studies requirement – really quite a good idea to prevent over-specialisation at too early a stage. A number of new instructors were recruited, ground and air, and those parts of the old AST not needed were bought up by Airwork and transferred to their base at Perth. For a few months the last of the old AST students (including one of mine, Hoosain Arif, a Burmese who is now a training Captain on Malta Airlines) finished their training alongside the new cadets, who began with a short grading course on the Chipmunks.

We were now authorised to do our own Civil Aviation Authority flight tests, and no longer had to traipse up to Stansted for our instrument rating renewals on the CAA Consuls and Doves. It was a pretty heavy day to drive up from Southampton to Stansted, do the test, and get back, all in the same day. In today's modern air and road traffic conditions I doubt if it would be possible.

As part of our integration into the corporations we were sent on familiarisation flights on BEA. With a friend and colleague Peter Duff-Mitchell I flew in a BEA Viscount with a Captain Monro to Hamburg – down the corridor to Berlin, where we spent the night, and back the next day by the same route. I had two short spells in the right-hand seat. All very different from the last time I 'visited' Berlin 15 years previously.

My very last flight on the Oxford filled me with nostalgia. It was on the 23rd February 1961, some 20 years since my first. It also marked the last of the AST students.

Most of the early College flying was grading the first intake of new cadets. They were 1) young, 2) English, 3) most highly motivated, and 4) very rigorously selected. Life was now different; we had very few early failures, in fact few failures all along the line, but tragically one of my first four failed a medical and had to be given a ground job in the Corporation. He was devastated and I felt for him a great deal. If Chris Preece reads this he will remember. I believe he carved out a successful career in station management.

At first courses were sponsored by British European Airways or British Overseas Airways Corporation, but later of course they merged.

We had to recruit quite a lot of new staff and mostly these were ex-Service instructors, although not all. Many now who joined had no wartime experience, the originals were getting a bit long in the tooth! The College was officially opened on the 19th May 1961 by the Duke of Edinburgh. It was marked by a mass formation flypast by the College Chipmunks (nine, I think). I was in No. 2 position with a cadet called Riley, who later specialised in light aircraft aerobatics as well as carting 'heavy people carriers' around Europe!

I still managed to get an occasional Rapide flight, thanks to Viv Bellamy at Eastleigh. He was ex-Fleet Air Arm, did not suffer fools gladly and was a tremendous character. I must digress at this stage to pay him due tribute. We first met one night at Eastleigh when I was working for Marshall's and was landing there to clear customs for a party I had flown from Cambridge to the Channel Islands that day. Anyway, on a rather sedate base leg I was cut out by another

Rapide doing a very tight circuit: it was Viv. No hard feelings, we had to spend the night there anyway.

Since coming down to Hamble Viv had let me fly his Rapide to keep the type on my licence and I once recall taking eight vegetable pickers to Alderney and bringing back half a ton of potatoes. He married the charming Jane Fairey (the aircraft manufacturer's daughter, who had done some flying with us at AST) and the last time we met (in the late 1970s, I think it was) he showed me the Sopwith $1^1/_2$ Strutter he was rebuilding. The nicest thing he did to me was to take me up in his two-seat Spitfire VIII on the 17th July 1961. That I enjoyed; I had flown a Hurricane but never a Spit. I wonder where that aircraft is now, also the Gladiator he was rebuilding. But I did get a flight in his Currie Wot! Dear old Viv, one of *the* characters in aviation and at the time of writing just recently departed this world. If he is in heaven, as he deserves, I bet he is rebuilding old aeroplanes!

By November 1961 we had our fleet of Piper Apaches (later changed for the more virile and challenging Beechcraft Barons) and began the advanced stage of training. Hamble being a grass airfield, we badly needed runways, and we developed a very good working agreement with one of our neighbours, Lee-on-Solent, to use theirs. We also began a regular 'service' to Swansea using similar route cards to those in use at that time in BEA and taking non-flying employees as passengers. This was quite popular.

When the first course was completed and began their careers in the two corporations, I went down to Malta in a Vanguard (G-APET) with a training captain, Ron Gillman DFC DFM, crew and cadets for their first training flights in the aircraft they were to go on. It was a pleasant surprise to see how well they adapted. Apparently it was cheaper to take them down to Malta for their conversion training than to do it in the UK. Certainly they had good en route experience and a much more reliable weather factor. I spent three very interesting days on that detachment and also had an hour in the right-hand seat myself. It was good to see how well our ex-cadets adapted to the Vanguard, having only flown Chipmunks and Apaches up to then, although prior use of flight simulators had also been of very good value. We were pleased at the College that very few indeed of those who graduated could not cope with the exacting standards set up by BOAC and BEA.

We had two simulators at Hamble. They were not of any specific type but had the characteristics of a four-engined jet. One was programmed for the UK and one for the United States. Two cadets (Captain and First Officer) were supervised by an instructor and a fourth crew member who acted as Air Traffic Control and set up the aircraft on the runway. A typical training route on the US simulator would be from New York to Boston. It trained cadets to develop a clear mental picture of their environment and to cope with the higher speeds involved (the performance roughly equated to the Comet). Every approach and landing was on the ILS (Instrument Landing System), as this was in universal use and as a pilot-interpreted aid developed the mental picture they needed. All manner of failures and malfunctions could be induced, in fact care was needed not to unfairly overload an inexperienced crew to the point of breakdown.

I was giving a test, on one occasion, and detected a marked air of 'testitis,' so to try and reduce the tension I walked out of the flight deck and let them get on with it without breathing down their necks. I could monitor their progress very well at the operator's console where their position was being recorded on the master position indicator.

When I returned I said to the cadet captain: "Excuse me, but is your daughter a stewardess on this flight? There's a girl back there who looks very like you!" Thus does one try to set a hard-working cadet at ease.

Before selection for the course, which lasted for two years, the aspiring airline pilot had to have the equivalent (I think from memory) of five 'A' level GCEs, pass a medical and pass a flying grading test, which was some 3–4 hours in a Chipmunk. In the first year the elementary training alternated daily with ground school and liberal studies, an excellent mind-broadening exercise to give more depth to the cadets' general knowledge and personality. They were all as keen as mustard and knew how to work hard. Being so meticulously hand-picked and keen they were quite a contrast to the previous students we had at AST – at least to some of them.

Now as I write those on the first courses are themselves coming up to retirement. How time flies!

By August 1965 the College was looking for a replacement for the Apaches. Something faster and more virile was needed. So we had the pleasant task of evaluating suitable alternatives. We tested the Piper Aztec and Twin Comanche, Beechcraft Baron and Travelair and the Beagle 206. It was sad in a way that we could not give the thumbs-up to the sole British contender, the Beagle 206, but the final choice of the Baron was a good one. The Baron was fast, rugged, had an excellent single-engined performance and needed fine judgement operating in and out of Hamble, day and night. We flew it on airways all over the place – Northern Ireland, the Channel Islands and even Ronaldsway on the Isle of Man, a popular destination as there was room for a crate of good Manx kippers in the back!

In 1967 I transferred from being Flight Manager Advanced to become Flight Manager in charge of working up an intermediate trainer, one which would eventually replace the ageing Chipmunks and take over their function as well; this was the Piper Cherokee. In many ways this was sad, for the Chipmunk was a marvellous aircraft, a worthy successor to the Tiger Moth, but not in keeping with the tricycle undercarriage philosophy of modern aircraft. We did retain some Chipmunks, especially for grading the aspiring candidates for the course; but the Cherokee had modern instrumentation and radio aids, better all-weather characteristics and the advantage of four seats. Due to congestion at Hamble we made arrangements with the Duke of Richmond and Gordon to operate from Goodwood, so the whole flight, instructor and three students per aircraft, would depart from Hamble for the day and operate from there. The arrangement worked well, and we got much more runway experience, albeit on grass! Of course the first task was to convert and get the instructors type-rated. Once we got going it worked well and I do not recall any particular interference from bad weather.

One of the aircraft evaluated to replace the Chipmunks was the Beagle Pup, its main disadvantage being that it had only three seats. Personally I would have preferred it and to 'Buy British,' and although I liked the docile quality of the Cherokee I think the

Beagle was the better aircraft. It might have kept the company solvent if we had chosen it. Pity!

The Barons started to arrive in April 1968 and soon replaced the Apaches when the staff had completed their type conversions. The Baron was a splendid aircraft and an excellent practical means of training cadets to have confidence in entering and leaving controlled airspace, carrying out full airways training and making instrument approaches. I do not have any statistics or facts to corroborate but I believe the Corporation was well-satisfied with the finished product when they got into their real jobs, and failures in the Corporation itself were few and far between. (Just as well as the total investment in the finished product must have been astronomical!)

The 5th of July 1971 was a nostalgic day for me. Jock Mouatt, who had sent me on my first solo in 1936, was an Air Traffic Controller at Hurn and I was able to take him up in a Baron from there – it was 33 years since we had last flown together!

Because of the congestion at Hamble, the advanced flight and the two flight simulators transferred permanently to Hurn, so there was a lot of commuting by car and air between the two airfields.

By this time I was the third senior pilot on the staff, which was quite a numerous one, and one of my most unpleasant duties (fortunately very rare) was testing cadets considered not up to the high standards required by the course. We were all of us, of course, subjected to routine tests: medicals, instructors' renewal tests, instrument rating renewals, competency checks, etc. etc., which was as it should be since we also gave some of them to others. But the very worst thing of all was the debriefing of a student who had finally failed a 'scrub' test; of course one did not feel nearly as awful as the victim, but it always hurt me inwardly, even if it was really in the best interest of the student. There were a few cases where relief was one of the emotions, since the candidate had come to realise the profession was not for him. None of them were fools!

One little bit of nostalgia must be permitted here if I may. On the 12th November 1971 I gave Chipmunk G-AMUF a C. of A. test before it was sold off. I first flew it in 1952, and in May 1998 I saw it again, in perfect condition (bless its owner!) at a light aircraft rally at White Waltham. I can't describe how I felt!

Early the next year there was quite a shake-up at the College, with a new Principal (who had not been there all that long) deciding on a major re-organisation. I did not exactly relish the outlook and a quite generous financial inducement offered to staff who wished to terminate their employment encouraged me to accept it and get out. The end of an era (or so I thought) – October 1949 to the end of January 1972. $22^1/_2$ years was a fair stretch. I left Hamble with very mixed feelings. I would have been much happier if I could have seen into the future!

## CHAPTER 10

# GROUNDED: ACADEMIC INTERLUDE
## UNIVERSITY OF SOUTHAMPTON 1972-1973

I decided to look around for a ground job of some sort and I was fortunate enough to apply for work at the University of Southampton, where there was a vacancy for an administrative assistant in the Department of Extra-Mural Studies (as it was then called). To my surprise I got the job and started in the bitterly cold winter of 1972, complete with power cuts and austerity. I had a lot to learn, and quickly, if I was to justify myself; there could not have been a greater contrast to my previous existence. I was given a tiny office and a nice secretary, and although dead worried at making a ghastly gaffe I knuckled under and learned as I went along. The work ethos was in complete contrast from the rather formal interactions among the staff at Hamble. I found it hard to call the head of department by his Christian name, and what an interesting lot they all were too! All colours of the political spectrum, and they all seemed to realise my political neutrality; and some would occasionally confide in me about each others' political leanings!

One of my first embarrassments was to disclose that my wife and I had been given a gift holiday of a free first-class return flight on a VC.10 to Fiji for two weeks, which they generously allowed me to take. It was a marvellous experience and I spent quite a bit of time on the flight deck; the route was New York–Los Angeles–Hawaii–Fiji, and Fiji was absolutely out of this world; we thoroughly enjoyed ourselves and it was good to have a job to go back to, even if the pay was less than half of my College salary. I remember being in a staff conference the day after I got back suffering terrible jet lag. Again their tolerance was out of this world.

As I got used to the life I settled down, organising supplies, classrooms, lectures, etc. I even laid on a series of my own (on flying of course!) which was quite well attended. But – and there always seems to be a 'but'! – I found as I got more on top of the job that I missed flying like hell (not alleviated by being able to hear some of the aircraft traffic around Eastleigh from my open office window).

In June 1973 Wendy Aspden (née Sabberton of Cambridge days of 1947–48) took me up in a Cessna 150 G-BAEV from Eastleigh. We did spins, aerobatics and circuits: the aviation bug had been reawakened.

In July I went back to Eastleigh and got Tony Liskutin, the CFI there, to renew my licence for me. Dear old Tony, a gallant Czech pilot if ever there was one – he used to be with me at Hamble. In October I gave flights to my secretary, Sue Willgoss, and to a couple of other University friends, and at the end of September I resigned and went on the dole! How rash can you get? But the children were all independent and Jean bravely and tolerantly supported me.

So I drew the dole for a while and had no qualms about it either. I had contributed in taxes all my working life, after all. Thankfully my faith in the future was vindicated because in December on a visit back to Hamble I renewed my instructor's rating. It transpired that they were short of staff and could do with my services, would I care to come back? Would I just! On the 9th April 1974 Wendy and I had a nostalgic flight from Eastleigh to Cambridge and the next day I started work again at Hamble.

## CHAPTER 11
# GOING ROUND AGAIN
### FLYING AT EASTLEIGH AND HAMBLE 1973-1984

Prior to starting again Hamble renewed my instrument rating on the Baron. The CFI who tested me used to be my deputy flight manager in the old days, but I did not mind a bit being just an ordinary instructor. No longer did I have to sign on in the dole queue and over the years the pay was better than when I left.

I started work on the 9th April 1974 on the Chipmunk and Cherokees, and this Indian Summer extended to a total of ten months. But from February to July 1975 I was out of work again. However, I renewed my contacts at Eastleigh and began work there on the 22nd July, flying Cessna 150s. This again was a new environment, both in the air and on the ground; a club instructor (and even the CFI, which I eventually became) was a very different animal from a corporation-employed professional. Hours and conditions of service were very different, and fitting in flying instruction from a very busy commercial airport was much more stressful than operating from a private airfield.

Half the money, twice the workload and just as much basic pleasure and satisfaction with the progress of one's students, and very different some of them were: ATC cadets on flying scholarships, ladies past their first flush of youth, a few ex-pilots, all keenly motivated. The two-seat Cessna 150s we used were fully aerobatic and very rugged, not as roomy nor as comfortable as the Cherokee, but very light on the controls and excellent for their purpose. We also had a Cessna 172 for aerial work and charter, of which we did quite a lot, including photography.

Soon after I began work there, an Air Training Corps flying scholarship contract necessitated my taking 'EV, in April 1976, up to CFS, then at Little Rissington, to get their approval of me as the CFI. I remember getting there with a lot of difficulty through a weather front, but fortunately it cleared before I got there and all went well – it was quite late by the time I got back. Five days later I sent my first ATC cadet on his first solo.

The 20th August 1976 was a celebration day as my eldest son Trevor (the vet), recently back from working in Australia, came down to Eastleigh (he had flown Chipmunks in Liverpool University Air Squadron) and I had the pleasure of sending him solo in the Cessna 150. However he did not have the time to give up to flying as he was setting up a very busy veterinary practice in Acton. That August was a very busy month as I logged 80 hours' flying.

So the weeks and months went by. It was frustrating at times trying to give dual to very varied qualities of trainees, fitting departures, arrivals and circuits in a very busy commercial airfield with a single runway. But I had excellent back-up from George Watts and his wife, who did all the admin, and from keen young instructors who were anxious to build up their hours and experience before going on to better-paid work in the airlines. It was all so totally different to Hamble, probably even more challenging. I loved the diversity of club members, all keen, some working very hard to save their pennies to go flying (having been in their shoes when I first learned I appreciated their situation). After $3^1/2$ years I had had enough.

I had, in May 1978, paid a short visit to Hamble where the Chief Flying Instructor, Tommy Thompson, had once in the past been my deputy flight manager and who had renewed my instrument rating some four years previously, but on this occasion he said that it would not be necessary as he did not think I would be needed for much more than six weeks or so, and I would be on basic training. That was OK by me, and now with hindsight the whole thing was a miracle, the six weeks stretched out for nearly three years – until the end of January 1981! It was my second Indian Summer – a well-paid five-day week, no night-flying, excellent students and good friends among all the staff, including some of the engineers I had known since Watchfield days of 40 years before – and excellent they all were, the serviceability rate was outstanding. What more could a 60-year-old want?

They refrained from calling me grandad (although of course by now I was one!); however the Corporation (now British Airways) was completing its needs for pilots for the foreseeable future and numbers began to dwindle. We had one course of pilots for – I think – Britannia Airways, and some came in from a few other state airlines, among them Zambia, so we were almost back to the old days of Air Service Training. A few of my students at this time were ex-ATC cadets I had helped to train initially in the flying school at Eastleigh some years before.

The 16th October 1979 was a day to savour as it was 30 years ago to that day that I had first started work at Hamble. I was the last instructor remaining from those days! In December 1979 I was allocated the first BA cadet of the opposite sex as a student. Diana Barton had good previous experience, she had obtained an instructor's endorsement on her private pilot's licence at an aero club and was no problem whatsoever. A few years ago I heard on the grapevine that she had obtained her captaincy in British Airways and clearly she had an excellent career still ahead of her! I would dearly love to know how she is getting on.

The 28th January 1980 was another nostalgic day for me (the longer one lives the greater is that emotion!) as I flew over to Sandown in the Isle of Wight and had a very pleasant reunion with the well-known (but of course now retired) professional aerial photographer, Cyril Peckham, who had come down to Hamble 28 years previously to carry out some aerial photography (see Chapter 8). We got a mention and a photo in the local Isle of Wight paper. It was good meeting him again.

On the 25th November 1980 I gave a student a long dual cross-country to Lands End, as I had never been there. My old friend from early days, Viv Bellamy, was there and we had lunch together and a good old nostalgic yarn. He showed me a Sopwith $1^1/_2$ Strutter he was rebuilding. I never found out if he completed it and the next time I heard about him was 18 years later, when sadly he took off for circuits and aerobatics in another world. We did not meet often in life, but when my number is up I shall hope for another reunion!

So time went by and in January 1981 I left for the third and last time the airfield and the work I loved so much. I was terribly sad, but the flying school at Eastleigh was still there, and after another wonderful (and first class!) free ride with BA to Hong Kong and back in February and March, I returned to the flying school and resumed work again much as before. However, work there was also slowing down; I could sense I was on final approach. After a moderately busy April in 1982, in the next three months things ground to a halt, and my last flight as a commercial pilot/instructor was on the 8th July. I wonder if my very last student, Joan Reed of J.J. & J. Reed, sewing machine vendors, remembers it?

CHAPTER 12
# WEATHER AND OTHER MISCELLANEA

*"The Time has come, the met man said,*
*To say how smart we are*
*To talk of cold occluded fronts*
*And kink the isobar,*
*And tell you how we know for sure*
*At stroke of two 't'will clear.*
*'We doubt it,' said the pilots all*
*And shed a bitter tear."*

(from "The Weather Eye," 1942, – author unknown – with apologies to Lewis Carroll)

Ever since my early experience trying to reach Lympne in deteriorating weather, as related in Chapter 1, I have always been very weather-conscious as it plays a major part in aviation. Meteorology is a fascinating subject and weather was much less accurately predicted until fairly recently. My experience in bad weather approaches at Watchfield and Shawbury and the vital part weather played during operations kept it in the forefront of my mind as it probably did everybody else's.

I have had several lucky scrapes and/or narrow squeaks during my career. But flying above broken cumulus in the dear old Tiger, 'hedge-hopping,' and steep-turning around cloud tops with only occasional glimpses of the ground was an exhilarating experience; this was especially so when one met the shadow of one's aircraft surrounded by a completely circular rainbow on the side of a towering cumulus cloud. Also 'hedge-hopping' along the top of a level sheet of stratus in winter and then letting down into the winter gloom below was an experience to be relished, not least finding where one was.

Oh! happy carefree days, abolished forever after about 1950 with the advent of radio, controlled airspace, and instrument ratings. Those of us who flew prewar in the UK, with virtually no radio, no controlled airspace and many fewer aircraft lived in an almost fairytale world. Think of it! No airways, no London Zone, only limited airfield traffic zones and virtually no speech radio – W/T yes, R/T no. Heaven!

To sum it up, may I tell the wartime story of the Anson pilot on a delivery flight who got lost in bad weather. He had a navigator-cum-wireless operator, but was thoroughly caught out flying low in cloud. He asked urgently for a fix and after what seemed like ages the navigator came up to the cockpit and tapped him on the shoulder.

"Where are we, then?" asked the pilot.

"Take your helmet off," said the navigator; "according to my calculations you are now under the dome of St. Paul's Cathedral."

It's not like that any more!

This brings me to talk briefly of the early days of open cockpits and helmet-and-goggles flying. Before the installation of electric intercom in the Tiger Moths of Training Command (which came in about the early 1950s, I think) the art of communication between a pilot and passenger (instructor and pupil) was by the first-war invention of Gosport Tubes; these were flexible tubes with a mouthpiece and two earpieces which plugged into the helmets that were worn. The art of giving good clear flying instruction using these was very much an acquired one, particularly when 'pattering' (as it was called) aerobatics. Manoeuvres of positive 'g' were not much problem but slow rolls and inverted flight made keeping the mouthpiece in place very difficult, as the left hand had to be on the throttle and the right hand on the stick (we didn't give it the high-falutin' name of control column in those days!). So the only way was to lodge it in the cleft of one's chin. I was lucky I had a suitable one in mine!

Another fundamental change as far as I was concerned was the anxiety state engendered not only in the pupil, but also in the instructor, on sending a first solo. Altogether I sent 124 first solos and initially I was probably as worried about it as the student, especially having to stand and watch helplessly while it took place; however in my case all went well (excepting the tragic first-night solo in 1941 as previously mentioned). However, the problem has been dramatically eased by the introduction of virtually universal tricycle undercarriages in most (if not all) basic training aircraft. These are notably easier to land than the old 'tail-draggers' of the past. Not a bad thing, I suppose, but still a matter of nostalgic pride lost by modern rationalisation. Tricycle undercarriages have been used from earliest times and it is perhaps surprising that they weren't developed more from the very beginning.

Incidentally there was an interesting case of a first solo at Cambridge in the late 1940s when a student in a Tiger on a first solo did, I believe, some seven slight bounces and go-arounds before finally coming safely to rest!

To me, one of the more responsible tasks as an instructor was sending off a first solo cross-country, especially before aircraft were equipped with radio, when help could be given. Not only the pupil's flying ability but weather considerations played a significant part, and later on, of course, there was the risk of inexperienced pilots violating controlled airspace. Again the advent of radio reduced this problem, but often I would wait and worry more about a student on a first solo cross-country than on a first solo. When I was at Hamble the problem was eased because a student could be briefed, if hopelessly lost, to steer south to the coast and then fly along it, east or west, to reach home!

Which brings me to airfields. Altogether I have landed at 304 different airfields, landing grounds and occasionally the odd farmer's field to retrieve lost students (not invariably mine!). Our cross-country route for the Commercial Pilot Licence (200 nautical miles with two away-landings) was Hamble–Weston-super-Mare–Lympne–Hamble. So foreign students had it as easy as we could make it. Even so, with no radio, there were problems and I once had to retrieve an Arab from a field where he had made a precautionary landing which was, in fact, in sight of Lympne!

All in all I flew as pilot in charge in 67 different types and three gliders; as second pilot a further 10 and two gliders. Which did I enjoy the most? A difficult question, but undoubtedly, although I only flew it three times briefly, the Southern Martlet was *the* fun plane. The Mosquito was the best twin (and the best twin, in my experience, with one engine feathered!). I loved the Airspeed Oxford, a brute to fly until one got used to it, but a marvellous trainer, as was the Tiger Moth, but that wasn't a brute to fly, it was simply a marvellous trainer. But to my regret I never had a chance to fly a Stampe which I suspect was better than the Tiger Moth.

The modern tricycles don't do much for me, Cherokees, Apaches, Cessna 150s and 172s; they are all right but seem to me to lack what my old French master called *élan*! Bread-and-butter pudding but completely in tune with their times. The Cessna 150 was reasonably manoeuvrable but I hated the high wing over my head.

Going back to the later twin-engine tricycle undercarriage trainers, my vote went to the Beechcraft Baron, which had excellent twin handling, a fast performance and a first-class performance with one engine feathered. It proved an excellent trainer for basic handling and airways experience for the Hamble cadets.

I still have an ambition to fly in a balloon, but also I would dearly have loved to go up in an airship. When I was young they were still regarded as a possible substitute for the ocean liner and I believe the last German airship was briefly used against us in the last major war. With modern technology and safer lifting gas several small airships are operated, mostly in the United States. It would round off my career nicely to get up in the sharp end of one!

## CHAPTER 13
# RUNNING DOWN CHECKS
## DOWN TO EARTH AT LAST (NO MORE MEDICALS!) 1984-1998

So it was all over – no more half-yearly medicals, no more instructor renewals, no more competency checks, no more type ratings! It is said that flying is the most tested profession and it is right that it should be. It is safer than driving, *and* more rewarding, and I missed it like hell. However, I still had a few log book entries as unofficial unpaid second pilot, the first of which was in August 1984 when Malcolm Mayes, a glider pilot whom I had converted to power-flying at Eastleigh, took me up in an RS.28 sailplane on a glider tow at Thruxton up to 2,500 feet and we had 55 minutes of glorious soaring. The last time I had done that sort of thing was in a Kranich at Cambridge in June 1948, 36 years previously.

A near-neighbour, Barry Nicholson, gave me several memorable flights in his Grob, G-BMGR, a fantastic powered glider which used its engine in lieu of a glider tug, feathered the airscrew and then became a sailplane. It was equipped with all mod cons, R/T, ADF, VOR, etc, and was based at Lasham. One August day we went on a cross-country and, returning to Lasham, Barry feathered the engine and flew over the burning stubble (the harvest was just over), and in some accurate steep turns proceeded to gain height in the thermals that the heat had generated. I certainly admire and respect those who go aviating for long durations and distances in motorless aircraft. I shall go for soaring if I get the chance in another life!

On another occasion, when quite by chance I happened to read in a flying book that the Southern Martlet, G-AAYX, that I had flown in 1936, was at Old Warden about to begin restoration (this was now 1989), Barry and I flew up and I showed them my log book for 1936 and photographs. I am still in touch with Shuttleworth and at the time of writing, some nine years later it has still not yet been completely restored! When it is, another ambition will be fulfilled if I can get up there again to see it.

At this stage of my story, perhaps a brief family and sporting dissertation to round off the non-flying side of my existence is in order.

My father, mother and stepmother and their assorted offspring all shared a love of golf. My family were members of a very pleasant club called Hengrove, not far from Margate, and I started out there with sawn-off wooden clubs from a very young age. Some of my happiest golfing memories are of that idyllic place, which was requisitioned soon after 1939 and ploughed up – sacrilege! It has never been restored, more's the pity. I can recall every one of its 18 holes as if it were yesterday. Just before I went abroad I flew over it in the Hornet Moth and put my father off his putt on the fourth green. Not much he could do about it either, as soon afterwards I left the country!

I had the chance of very few games during and after the war, but when we moved down from Cambridge in 1949 I tried out all the local courses and joined Hockley Golf Club near Winchester, as it was as near to the spirit of dear old Hengrove as one could get. The course and the members are all splendid and I have spent many happy hours there, albeit with some nostalgia as it lies under the approach to runway 20 at Eastleigh and I find it hard to keep my eye on the ball when aircraft fly over on the approach, as indeed I have often done myself, once with three other club members as passengers in a Cessna 172. Professional etiquette has prevented me from ever landing on it (the eleventh fairway is very suitable!) much as I would have liked to.

My elder brother Pat was a much better golfer than me – handicap 8 – and when he retired to England from South America he brought a house within reach of the championship courses at Deal and Royal St. Georges in Kent and I spent many happy holidays with him and his charming wife and daughter, playing those courses. In spite of the great levelling of the handicapping system I never remember beating him. He departed this world recently and as he was eight years older than I am he had set me another target to reach!

As to my family, what can I say? The photo of us all gives the complete gathering at our Golden Wedding in 1991 (except for one charming Yugoslavian daughter-in-law who was in bed with a temperature of 100° – the other equally charming daughters-in-law are French and English!). We are quite an international family as our daughter has very bravely adopted a Vietnamese and a Guatemalan boy. She and her wonderfully supportive husband live and work in the South of France so we don't often see them.

Three years to go to our Diamond Wedding, fingers crossed! Perhaps this is a suitable stage to pay due tribute to my wonderful wife Jean who has bravely and stoically battled against ill health for many years, yet remains steadfast and cheerful and most supportive of all my comings and goings. As mentioned earlier she instinctively hated flying, so all the more credit to her for taking me on and sticking with it.

Every so often I meet up with, or hear about, some of my friends and colleagues from the past; these are priceless jewels in the crown of one's experience of life. Perhaps a couple of examples will serve to explain.

In 1990 we moved into a block of flats in Winchester, and in the course of meeting the other residents, one of them said to me, when she heard that I had trained British Airways pilots: "Did you know Richard X?"

I could not recall the name, but she said not to worry, he was her son-in-law and she was visiting him that evening as he was at home ('resting between trips,' it was sometimes called) and she would ask him. Shortly after we got back to our flat she phoned and told me that her son-in-law knew me very well, as I had given him his final College flying test in the Baron, and on completion I had said to him: "That's OK, you can take my wife up any time you like!"

Of course, I was able to verify the date by reference to my log book.

On another occasion about ten years ago I was playing in a 'seniors' golf match at Hockley against the Royal Winchester seniors. It was a four-ball competition and one of the opponents in my match was none other than Peter Sleight, ex-Flight Lieutenant 105 Squadron whom I had not seen since 1945, 40 years previously! We managed to recognise each other; he had joined British South American Airways (founded by our late AOC Donald Bennett), which was eventually merged into BOAC/BA. Like me, he was of course retired, and I had no idea he lived locally. We do have occasional Hamble and RAF reunions but I have not had the opportunity to attend – in any case it's too far in the past now.

A couple of years back I was briefly in touch with my old chief at Cambridge, Sir Arthur Marshall; he is now on economical cruising as he is a nonagenarian!

Two more flying memories complete my odyssey. In June 1993 I went with my second son, Clive, to Compton Abbas to hire a plane to survey his home near Sherborne. The pilot was none other than my friend and ex-Hamble colleague Alec Blythe, an ex-RAF Group Captain whom I had checked out in the Chipmunk many years previously when he joined the staff at Hamble. And the aircraft? None other than a Cherokee Warrior, G-BPCK. Alec just sat back and I was able to prove that judgement and technique had not diminished with the passage of time. That was the 2nd June 1993.

The next occasion was on the 3rd June 1998 when again we visited Compton Abbas for another aerial view, and guess what! Yes, it was Cherokee G-BPCK once again, but by now Alec had retired. However the charming young pilot (they are all young now to me!) had possibly heard of me. Anyway he handed over to me before take-off and I was able to justify his confidence in me.

My third flight two days later did not go so well – the weather was foul and the pilot critical. Since then time will tell if I ever get another chance. One ambition has not yet been fulfilled. That last time, at my request, Clive had arranged a family outing in a balloon, but it was (quite rightly) cancelled for weather. I continue to live in hope! But time is running out; having joined the ranks of the octogenarians I need to lower my expectations as well as my undercarriage!

However, in May last year I managed to get to the vintage light aircraft rally at White Waltham. It was almost a surfeit of nostalgia. An Auster III (of Cambridge days, 1945), Hornet Moths, the lovely little Chilton that I met at Ramsgate in the 1930s and never managed to get airborne in, and, lo and behold, none other than Chipmunk G-AMUF that I knew from Hamble days in the fifties to seventies, looking resplendently young and well cared for. I never got to meet the owner, Ian Mills, but via a mutual friend, Peter

Campbell, he has generously offered me a flight in it. So I am hoping to get to this year's event at Kemble (of nostalgic memory) as there may well be a chance to indulge in an enormous bout of nostalgia; but it's daunting to realise that I am twice the age of that aeroplane!

I will conclude with a short work of fiction, an article I wrote in "*Astra*," the house magazine of Air Service Training, in 1950; it could be an appropriate way of concluding my story.

Only the title needs amendment. I badly misjudged the dear old Tiger Moth. By entitling the article "Nostalgia – 1960" I gravely shortened the life of that wonderful aeroplane. Thanks to devoted *aficionados*, dozens of Tigers still fly and will see the millennium in. I did over 1,900 hours on it and should have known better. It's odds on now that the Tiger Moth will see me out!

## CHAPTER 14
# "NOSTALGIA – 1960"

"The old man's faded eyes gazed with ardent longing. He hadn't been young when he flew the very first Tiger Moth at the old Stag Lane Aerodrome in '32 – or was it '33? He was getting too old to remember much these days, anyway, but the sight of a biplane still flying revived a crowd of happy memories. Service with a Reserve School before the Nazi war (the Tiger was the *élite* of trainers in those days, as the Chipmunk had been in the fifties), six glorious months as CFI at Wincaster and the change-over to uniform when the war came. The 'bind' of grading, the welcome change in Canada to Tigers with hoods, brakes and a tailwheel. He had been cheesed off after 10 years in Tigers but remembered with sadness his posting home, not knowing when he would fly in one again.

Then he recalled the struggle to keep flying during the uneasy years of the phoney peace until the final realisation came that he was too old for it, when he failed his medicals and was politely but firmly turned away when the Communist war broke out.

Now there it was again, a real DH.82A Tiger Moth, its Gipsy Major engine ticking over smoothly whilst the mechanic waited for it to warm up.

Why should fate have brought him into contact with a Tiger again after so many years? How he longed to climb in again and do one more circuit! Surely after 3,000 hours on a type he wouldn't have forgotten anything? He peered about him; the only mechanic was now strolling over to sign the certificate – nobody was about.

Without further thought he slipped the chocks away and with some difficulty heaved his weary joints up into the rear cockpit. Automatically checking trim fully back, slats locked and friction nut slack, he glanced up at the gauge and noticed a full tank. Opening the throttle and looking around, he moved forward and turned out on to the field feeling a grim thrill of pleasure which set his heart thumping madly inside him, contracting his stomach until he felt almost sick with mingled fear and elation.

Much too fast, fearing pursuit, he taxied over to the lee side of the field, doing his take-off check on the way (how often had he reprimanded his pupils for doing them like that instead of stopping crosswind to do it!). Without pausing, except for an instinctive look downwind, he turned and opened up for the take-off. It hadn't occurred to him how blustery it would be without a helmet and he was glad of his glasses for the protection of his eyes from the fury of the slipstream. As the tail came up he suddenly felt himself swing to the right (how easily he forgot that would happen) and automatically put on left rudder to correct it; so, hardly before he knew what was happening, he found himself airborne and climbing up into a deep blue sky, blotted here and there with the dark and sinister undersides of thunder clouds building up in the warm July sunshine.

His heart had slowed down now and he suddenly realised the enormity of his offence – he had stolen an aircraft in a spirit of sheer bravado and just to see if he could fly after a twelve years' break, and he an old man over seventy, too. He should have known better.

He looked down and saw again the sights he had long since forgotten which now returned to full flood of memory. How miniature it all looked from 1,000 feet; tiny houses and fields, the beauty of the woods and of the sun shining on the cathedral roof a full 10 miles distant! His spirit was once more raised to a peak of joyousness – he was airborne again! What a tale he would be able to tell his friends when he got down and how he would gloat over yet another entry (however unauthorised) in his log book when he got home!

Looking around, as he turned, he searched with difficulty for the airfield, finally locating it after a moment's panic – he hadn't appreciated how defective his eyesight had become as his years increased. He began to think about his approach and landing. Up to now it hadn't worried him but doubt began to work its way into his mind and deflated the balloon of his first flush of over-confidence. Now he realised with a horrible certainty that he did not know whether he could land or not and his hand started to clench on the stick, his feet were jammed solid on the rudder bar and his whole body went rigid with fear and apprehension. A spasm of physical pain shot through him, though he scarcely noticed it, so much was he in the grip of his emotional stress. Now again he knew how so many of his students must have felt – yes, indeed, he himself on more than one occasion when he was learning. But how he envied them their advantages: youth, physical perfection, keenness, no sense of guilt; how enormously, he thought, his one advantage of experience was outweighed by these! How he regretted the times he had shouted at his pupils, his temper frayed, failing to appreciate how they felt at the time.

Almost by instinct he began to pray (though it was many years since he had done so), like a terrified child running to its mother for protection. His brain cleared as if his prayer had been answered (or was it instinct again?), and he remembered the vital actions before landing. Also he realised he was frozen on the controls and by a tremendous effort of will he let them go and checked the trim carefully.

Feeling like a man poised on the brink of a bottomless sea of icy water, reluctant to plunge in, he turned on to his approach, closing the throttle and easing back the trimmer. As the noise of the motor died away he peered toward the lee side of the field, trying to assess the drift and judge his height. Turning in to land he was suddenly aware that he was much too slow, the slats were hanging out and control was getting sloppy. Hastily he put the stick forward to regain speed, then, uncertain of his height again, he began to sideslip to the left, saw he was undershooting and gave a burst of throttle, hanging his head out to try to see how close he was to the boundary. The slipstream caught him full in the face and with a jerk wrenched his spectacles off, leaving him short-sighted and helpless at 100 feet over the boundary.

So this was how it must end, he thought, alone and helpless, but he would go out the way he had always wanted to, literally in harness! Instinctively he levelled out, peering at the cockpit instruments in an icy calm, so much in contrast to his downwind panic. He would show them he could do it, at least he could read his instruments. The altimeter read 50 feet now – he eased on 1,200 revs, keeping his speed at 50 knots. Sweating with fear but still controlling himself and the aircraft, he held on and waited, every split second an agonising decade of hope and fear . . .

Warned by the mechanic, the controller had pressed the crash bell and, unnoticed by the old man, the smooth organisation of the airfield's crash system went into action.

The CFI looked grimly out of his office window – so some stupid old fool had pinched his beloved Tiger, the last one flying, possibly the last biplane in existence – choice epithets arose in his mind, how he would tear him off an enormous strip when he got him into the office.

Out on the field the crash wagon waited, the ambulance with its doctor and orderlies began to tear across the field, heedless of the instructions not to obstruct the landing run. The driver saw the Tiger approaching head-on and stopped, remembering it was better to stay still, but too late, not knowing the plight of the pilot . . .

The old man turned across wind and taxied slowly back, switched off and climbed out. He had never remembered such a wonderfully smooth landing, one of those exquisite merges into the ground, with only the sound to tell him that contact had been made. Light of foot now and curiously finding his eyesight improved despite his loss of glasses, he walked into the tower, wondering at the strange quiet all around him.

Climbing the stairs, he walked into the office. There, the CHIEF PILOT gave him a look of deep and infinite love and compassion.

"Welcome home at last," he said, "We are proud to have you join us!"

Stammering his thanks and amazement, the old man looked around him and then out of the window. Twelve Tigers stood running up at the chocks, the sun shone down from a cloudless sky of infinite clarity, the windsock flapped idly from its pole and there, in the office, were his friends of 20, 30, yes, of 40 years ago."

And so, cleared to land, we are on finals. Good, a nice smooth touchdown and we turn off the runway and park in dispersal. Final cockpit checks done, operate the slow-running cutout. The engines stop and the only sounds are the clicks as they cool down. Back to the flight office, discuss minor snags with chiefie (RAF Flight Sergeant) and sign the form 700. Do we walk away without a backward glance? No, we give one final look back to what gave us a wonderful life – the aeroplane.

# APPENDIX 1

## AVIATORS CERTIFICATE

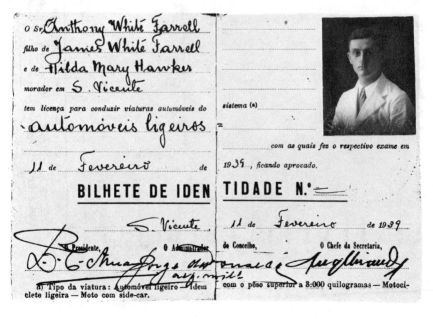

**Fédération Aéronautique Internationale British Empire.**

We the undersigned, recognised by the F.A.I. as the sporting authority in the British Empire certify that

Nous soussignés, pouvoir sportif reconnu par la F.A.I. pour l'Empire Britannique certifions que

Anthony White Farrell.

Born at London on the 5:11:1917

having fulfilled all the conditions stipulated by the F.A.I. has been granted an
AVIATORS CERTIFICATE.

ayant rempli toutes les conditions imposées par la F.A.I. a été breveté
PILOTE - AVIATEUR.

THE ROYAL AERO CLUB OF THE UNITED KINGDOM.

_____ Chairman.
_____ Secretary.
Date 30th June 1936 No 14011.

AVIATORS CERTIFICATE
ISSUED BY
The ROYAL AERO CLUB
119 PICCADILLY
LONDON, W.I.

## PORTUGUESE DRIVING LICENCE

O Sr. Anthony White Farrell
filho de James White Farrell
e de Hilda Mary Hawker
morador em S. Vicente

tem licença para conduzir viaturas automóveis do
automóveis ligeiros

sistema (a)

com as quais fez o respectivo exame em

11 de Fevereiro de 193? , ficando aprovado.

**BILHETE DE IDENTIDADE N.º**

S. Vicente                11 de Fevereiro de 1939

O Presidente,          O Administrador do Concelho,          O Chefe da Secretaria,

a) Tipo da viatura: Automóvel ligeiro — Idem com o pêso superior a 3:000 quilogramas — Motociclete ligeira — Moto com side-car.

87

# APPENDIX 2

## RECORDS OF MY CLIMBS
### 1) IN DH HORNET MOTH G-ADMM.

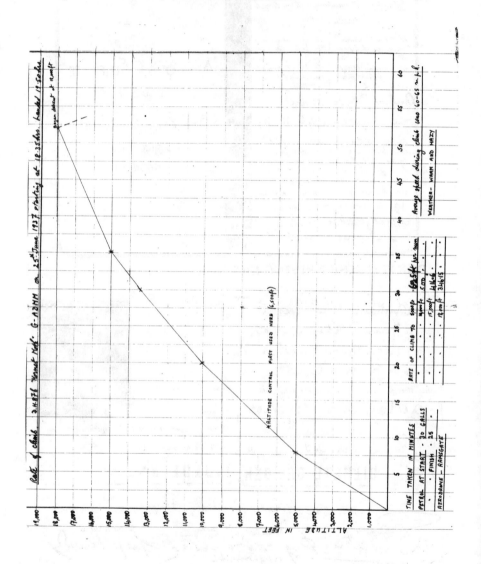

## 2) IN MILES MAGISTER G-AFEU

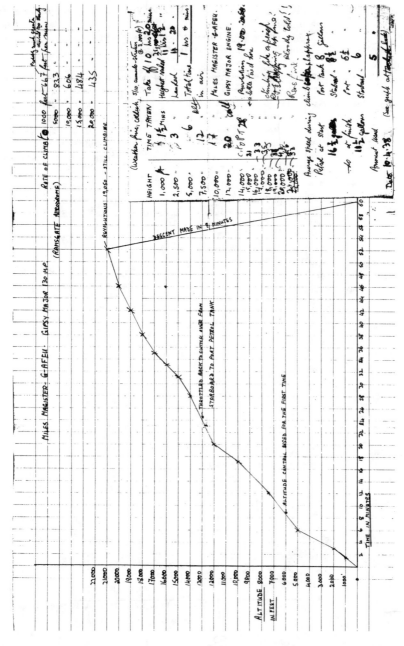

## 3) IN BA SWALLOW G-AERK

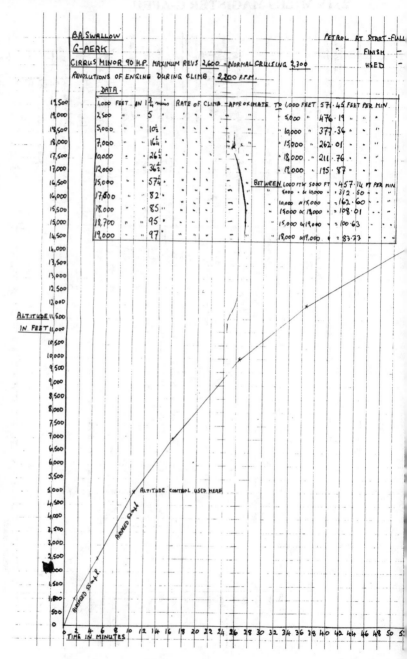

B.A. SWALLOW
G-AERK
CIRRUS MINOR 90 H.P. MAXIMUM REVS 2,600 - NORMAL CRUISING 2,300
REVOLUTIONS OF ENGINE DURING CLIMB - 2,200 R.P.M.

PETROL AT START - FULL
" " FINISH -
USED -

DATA.

| | | |
|---|---|---|
| 1,000 FEET IN 1¾ mins | RATE OF CLIMB - APPROXIMATE TO 1,000 FEET | 571·45 FEET PER MIN |
| 2,500 " " 5 " | " " " " 5,000 " | 476·19 " " |
| 5,000 " " 10½ " | " " " " 10,000 " | 377·34 " " |
| 7,000 " " 16¼ " | " " " " 13,000 " | 262·01 " " |
| 10,000 " " 26¼ " | " " " " 18,000 " | 211·76 " " |
| 12,000 " " 36¼ " | " " " " 19,000 " | 195·87 " " |
| 15,000 " " 57¼ " | | |
| 17,500 " " 82 " | BETWEEN 1,000 FT & 5000 FT = 457·14 FT PER MIN |
| 18,000 " " 85 " | " 5000 " & 10,000 " = 312·50 " " " |
| 18,700 " " 95 " | " 10,000 & 15,000 " = 162·60 " " " |
| 19,000 " " 97 " | " 15,000 & 18,000 " = 108·01 " " " |
| | " 15,000 & 19,000 " = 100·63 " " " |
| | " 18,000 & 19,000 " = 83·73 " " " |

ALTITUDE CONTROL USED HERE

AIRSPEED 50 m.p.h.

AIRSPEED 50 m.p.h.

ALTITUDE IN FEET

TIME IN MINUTES

90

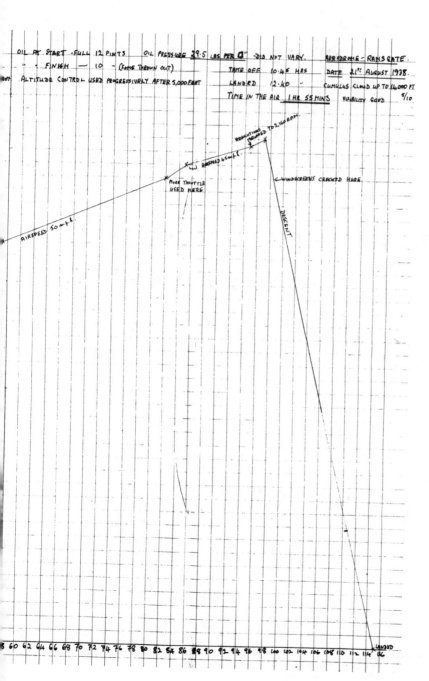

OIL AT START - FULL 12 PINTS    OIL PRESSURE 29.5 LBS PER ⎕" - DID NOT VARY.    AERODROME - RAMSGATE.
"   - FINISH  —  10  " (SOME THROWN OUT)    TAKE OFF   10.45 HRS    DATE 21ˢᵗ AUGUST 1938.
ALTITUDE CONTROL USED PROGRESSIVELY AFTER 5,000 FEET    LANDED   12.40 "    CUMULUS CLOUD UP TO 14,000 FT
                                                                    TIME IN THE AIR  1 HR 55 MINS    VISIBILITY GOOD    5/10

REVOLUTIONS DROPPED TO 2,160 R.P.M.

AIRSPEED 45 m.p.h.

MORE THROTTLE USED HERE

← WINDSCREENS CRACKED HERE.

DESCENT

AIRSPEED 50 m.p.h.

58 60 62 64 66 68 70 72 74 76 78 80 82 84 86 88 90 92 94 96 98 100 102 104 106 108 110 112 114 116    LANDED

91

# APPENDIX 3

## FIRST INTERNATIONAL "FLYING FLEA" CHALLENGE TROPHY RACE

## RAMSGATE AIRPORT LTD.

presents a

## GRAND AIR DISPLAY

and the

### 1st INTERNATIONAL

# " FLYING FLEA "

## CHALLENGE TROPHY RACE

(Under the Competition Rules of the Royal
Aero Club and Regulations of the F.A.I.)

— on —

## Monday, August 3rd, 1936

at 2-0 p.m.

---

OFFICIALS :

*Control Officers :*

Flight Lieut. C. E. ECKERSLEY-MASLIN *(Airport Manager).*
Flying Officer L. R. MOUATT.

*Marshals and Handicappers :* Capt. W. DANCY, F. ROWARTH

*Announcers :* J. L. BARNES, F. D. BRADBROOKE

*Organiser :* W. A. STREET

---

## PROGRAMME OF EVENTS

# FOREWORD.

The Operators of Ramsgate Municipal Airport are pleased to have this opportunity of showing Thanet the tremendous strides which Civil Aviation is making to-day.

In compiling the afternoon's Programme, endeavour has been made to present to the Public as many of the latest developments as possible, from the tiny "Pou du Ciel" of M. Mignet, the machine of the 'man in the street,' to the larger liners which operate so reliably in all parts of the world. Thus we aim at combining pleasant entertainment and interesting acquaintance with the transport which will soon be within the reach of all.

For the present, moreover, it can be enjoyed by anyone with the means and inclination for a pleasure flight in one of the several machines available for the purpose.

## SUMMARY OF TIME-TABLE (All times approximate)

| | | |
|---|---|---|
| 2-00 p.m. | Event No. 1. | Parade of participating machines. |
| 2-10 p.m. | Event No. 2. | Demonstrations of British machines by celebrated Pilots. |
| 3-00 p.m. | Event No. 3. | Landing Exhibition |
| 3-10 p.m. | Event No. 4. | " Flying Flea" Demonstration. |
| 3-30 p.m. | Event No. 5. | Parachute Descent. |
| 3-40 p.m. | Interval. | |
| 4-00 p.m. | Event No. 6. | "Flying Flea" Race |
| 4-45 p m. | Event No 7. | Aerobatic Display. |
| 5.00 p.m. | Event No 8 | Presentation of Prizes. |
| 5-15 p.m. till Dusk. | | Joy-riding by famous Pilots. |

NOTICE.—The Organisers cannot hold themselves responsible for the cancellation of any item on account of adverse circumstances, nor for any delay in the presentation of an item. Unexpected conditions cannot always be prevented.

## ACKNOWLEDGMENTS.

The Organisers would like to acknowledge their gratitude to the following for assistance :—

The Lady Mayoress (Mrs. H. Stead), for her consent to present the prizes.

Messrs. Dancy and Rowarth, for the Handicapping and Scrutineering of competing machines.

Messrs. Barnes and Bradbrooke, for announcements—pre-arranged and otherwise.

M. Mignet and Mr. S. V. Appleby, for expert advice.

The Owners and Pilots of all participating and visiting machines, for taking the air.

The Automobile Association, for Traffic Control.

The St. John Ambulance Brigade, for services rendered.

The Ramsgate Fire Brigade, for their very presence.

The Cleveland Petroleum Products Co., for their good spirit.

# ADVERTISEMENT FOR THE ABBOTT-BAYNES
## "CANTILEVER POU"

## THE
# ABBOTT—BAYNES
# "CANTILEVER POU"

Entirely redesigned Pou type Aeroplane, incorporating new features to give greater safety, strength and performance, including quickly detachable cantilever wings, no wires, positive controls, wing mass balancing and 30 h.p. Carden dual ignition engine.

SPECIFICATION: Span, 22ft. Weight empty, 327 lbs. Weight loaded, 550 lbs. Range, 200 miles. Maximum speed, 80 m.p.h. Cruising speed, 65 m.p.h. Climb, 400 ft. per minute.

PRICE COMPLETE. flight tested :

## £198

Including dual ignition, airspeed indicator, rev. counter, oil gauge, registration number.

Fitted with

## ·CARDEN

30 h.p. 4 Cylinder Aero Engine.

Price complete with Hub and Radiator

## £55

Dual Ignition £8-10-0 extra.

Specially designed for the Pou and ultra light 'planes, 4 cylinders, 4 stroke, giving a safety factor in flight which can never be approached by 2 cylinder types. Large reserves of power and practically vibrationless.

**ABBOTT-BAYNES AIRCRAFT,**
Branch of E. D. Abbott, Ltd.,
**Farnham, Surrey.**

**CARDEN AERO ENGINES Ltd,**
(controlled by Carden-Baynes Aircraft Ltd.)
**Heston Airport, Middlesex.**

# APPENDIX 4

## INVITATIONS TO THE OPENING OF RAMSGATE MUNICIPAL AIRPORT

RAMSGATE MUNICIPAL AIRPORT.

*Saturday, 3rd July, 1937.*

*Official Opening of the Airport by*

## Lt. Col. Sir FRANCIS C. SHELMERDINE, C.I.E., O.B.E.

DIRECTOR-GENERAL OF CIVIL AVIATION

*The Mayor of Ramsgate (Alderman Harry Stead, J. P.),*
*and Ramsgate Airport Limited,*
*request the pleasure of the company of*

*A. W. Farrell Esq.*

*at Luncheon at the Ramsgate Municipal Airport,*
*at 12.30 p.m. for 1 p.m. and afterwards to the Official Opening.*

R.S.V.P.
TOWN CLERK. RAMSGATE,
BY 29TH JUNE, 1937.

RAMSGATE MUNICIPAL AIRPORT.

*Saturday, 3rd July, 1937.*

*Official Opening of the Airport by*

## Lt. Col. Sir FRANCIS C. SHELMERDINE, C.I.E., O.B.E.

DIRECTOR-GENERAL OF CIVIL AVIATION

*The Mayor of Ramsgate (Alderman Harry Stead, J. P.),*
*and Ramsgate Airport Limited,*
*request the pleasure of the company of*

*A. W. Farrell Esq.*

*to the Official Opening of the Airport,*
*at 2.30 p.m. and afterwards to Tea.*

R.S.V.P.
TOWN CLERK. RAMSGATE,
BY 29TH JUNE, 1937.

AT THE ————————

# OFFICIAL OPENING

OF ————————

## RAMSGATE MUNICIPAL AIRPORT

ON

SATURDAY
3rd JULY, 1937

*Top: The Civil Air Ensign over the Terminal Building.*

*Centre: Demonstration by the Short Scion Senior.*

*Right: Polish in the Aircraft Park—a Hawker Hind.*

**THANET AIR DAY, SATURDAY, 21ST AUGUST 1937**

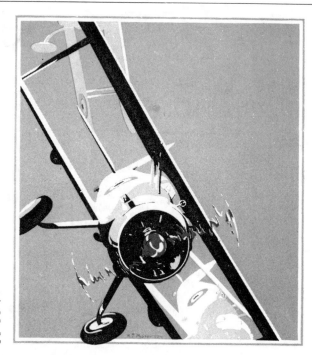

SOUVENIR
PROGRAMME
SIXPENCE

# THANET AIR DAY

## SATURDAY, 21ST AUGUST, 1937

RAMSGATE MUNICIPAL AIRPORT

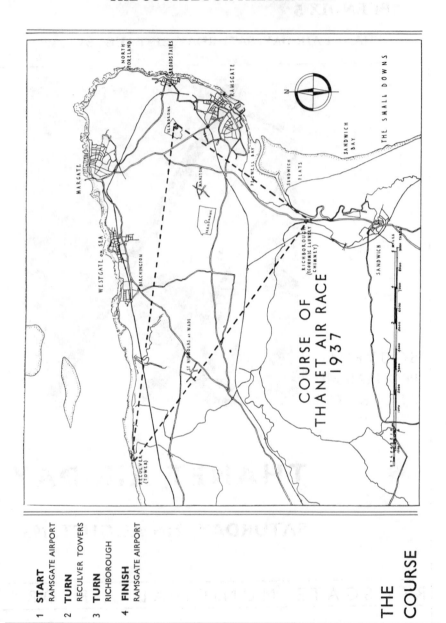

COURSE OF THANET AIR RACE 1937

1 **START** RAMSGATE AIRPORT

2 **TURN** RECULVER TOWERS

3 **TURN** RICHBOROUGH

4 **FINISH** RAMSGATE AIRPORT

THE COURSE

# ENTRANTS FOR THE AIR RACE

THANET AIR RACE, 1937

### Race Card.

| Aircraft | Registration | Pilot (Entrant) | Racing No. | Place | Speed m.p.h. |
|---|---|---|---|---|---|
| T.K.2. | G-ADNO | Geoffrey de Havilland (De Havilland Technical School) | 1 | | |
| B.A. Swallow | G-AERK | Miss G. Batchelor (A Batchelor) | 2 | | |
| V.E.F. 12 | YL-ABG | J. Vitols (LATVIAN) (ditto) | 3 | | |
| Mew Gull | G-AEXF | A. Henshaw (ditto) | 4 | 3rd | |
| Miles Whitney Straight | G-AEUX | J. Bayly (ditto) | 5 | | |
| Mew Gull | G-AEKL | C. Gardner (ditto) | 6 | | |
| Miles Hawk Special | G-ADGE | E.F. Walter (ditto) | 7 | | |
| Gipsy Moth | G-ADLJ | J.J.Flynn or M.Hymans (Paddy Flynn's Flying Club) | 8 | | |
| | | | 9 | | |
| | | | 10 | | |
| Gipsy Moth | G-ABOE | The Misses Glass. (Miss M. Glass) | 11 | | |
| Dart Kitten | G-AEXT | C.G.M.Alington (ditto) | 12 | | |
| Miles Whitney Straight | G-AEVA | M. Lazyo (ditto) | 14 | | |
| Spartan Arrow | G-ABOB | F/L H.R.A. Edwards (Lt.Col. L.A. Strange) | 15 | 2nd | |
| Taylor Cub | G-AESK | P.B. Elwell (A.J. Walter) | 16 | 1st | |
| Gipsy Moth | G-ABXR | R. Slazenger (ditto) | 17 | | |
| Avro 504 N | G-AIEV | P. Phillips (Air Publicity Ltd) | 18 | 4th | |
| Focke-Wulff F.W.56 | D-IMEQ | A. von Bohlen (Aero Club von Deutschland) | 19 | | |
| Klemm K.L.35 | D-EDLY | E. Gerbrecht (Aero Club von Deutschland) | 20 | | |
| Messerschmidt Me 27b | D-ESYR | W. Suwelack (Aero Club von Deutschland) | 21 | | |

99

## PATH FINDER FORCE BADGE

## ROYAL AIR FORCE

---

## PATH FINDER FORCE

---

### *Award of*
### *Path Finder Force Badge*

**This is to certify** that

### ACTING SQUADRON LEADER
### A. W. FARRELL. D.F.C., A.F.C. 85281

having qualified for the award of the Path Finder Force Badge, and
having now completed satisfactorily the requisite conditions of
operational duty in the Path Finder Force, is hereby

*Permanently awarded the Path Finder Force Badge*

Issued this **17th** day of **MAY** in the year 19**45**

*Air Officer Commanding, Path Finder Force.*

# APPENDIX 7

## DECOMPRESSION TEST RESULT

F/LT FARREL'S EFFORT - 20.000' SANS OXYGEN (SO FAR!)

8528   F/L

later 26 000 ft

91
84
87
83

26/4/
31-3-44.

Decompression chamber
up to 26.000' without
oxygen, passed out nearly,
revived as clever
figures show

83
82 ✗
81
79
77
75
73

# APPENDIX 8

## CARTOON (DRAWN BY A STUDENT ON THE 56 AOP COURSE, 22 EFTS, 10TH FEBRUARY 1947).

# APPENDIX 9

NO. OF HOURS ON COLLEGE SIMULATOR:     618

NO. OF PUPILS SENT ON FIRST SOLO:     124

NO. OF NATIONALITIES TRAINED:     31

These were from the following countries:

| | |
|---|---|
| America | Ireland |
| Brazil | Israel |
| Australia | Jordan |
| Belgium | Kuwait |
| Britain | Lebanon |
| Burma | Malawi |
| Canada | New Zealand |
| Cuba | Nigeria |
| Czechoslovakia | Norway |
| France | Persia |
| Germany | Poland |
| Gold Coast | Rhodesia |
| Holland | Saudi Arabia |
| Iceland | South Africa |
| India | Switzerland |
| Indonesia | |

# APPENDIX 10

## ANALYSIS OF FLYING BY TYPES
## (FROM 10/04/36–26/2/85)

N.B.: The aircraft are listed in order of my first flying in them. I'm afraid it would be more than I can manage to record all the serials of the aircraft I flew in during the war!

| TYPE | HOURS | REG. |
|---|---|---|
| AS P1 | | |
| DH.87B Hornet Moth | 98:00 | G-ADMM, G-ADFT, G-ADLY, G-ADOT, G-ADKC |
| Kronfeld Drone | 7:50 | G-AEEN |
| Hillson Praga | 1:25 | G-AEPI, G-AEUP, G-AEYL |
| Tipsy S.2 | 0:15 | G-AEWJ |
| BA Swallow (Cirrus) | 23:00 | G-AERK |
| Taylor Cub | 4:55 | G-AESK, G-AFFJ, G-AFFH |
| DH.60 Gipsy Moth | 0:55 | G-ABPK |
| Spartan Arrow | 7:05 | G-ABOB, G-ABWP |
| Miles Magister | 32:45 | G-AFEU |
| Southern Martlet | 0:35 | G-AAYX |
| Taylorcraft Model A | 0:10 | G-AFDN |
| Miles Whitney Straight | 64:35 | G-AFBV, G-AEVG |
| DH.82A Tiger Moth | 1914:45 | G-ADWG, G-AGZY, G-AHUB, G-AIBN, G-AHXN, G-AGYW, G-AKZL, G-AHXS, G-AKZM, G-AHVY, G-AHVX, G-ALND, G-AHWC, G-AHZK, G-ALWT, G-AHWA, G-AKZL, G-ACDI, G-AKZK, G-AHWB, G-ALWN, G-ALWU, G-ALWW, G-AHLB |
| DH.80 Puss Moth | 0:25 | G-ABWZ |
| Airspeed Oxford | 4464:20 | G-AITB, G-AITF, G-ALTP, G-ALTR, G-AIAX |
| Avro Tutor | 18:10 | |
| Avro Anson I & II | 18:10 | G-AHNS, G-AHNT |
| DH.89A Rapide & Dominie | 391:45 | G-AHED, G-AHLM, G-AGZO, G-ALWN, G-ALWL, G-ALWU, G-ANET, G-AFFB, G-AJHP, G-AJSL, G-AHGH, G-AHKB |
| Miles Master (I, II, III) | 4:00 | |
| Stinson Reliant | 0:25 | |

| | | |
|---|---|---|
| DH.98 Mosquito variants | | |
| (III, IV, XVI) | 427:55 | |
| Vickers Armstrong | | |
| Wellington X | 17.30 | |
| DH.94 Moth Minor | 1:00 | |
| Hawker Hurricane IIC | 0:30 | |
| Auster variants | 579:15: | |
| Taylorcraft Plus D | | G-AIIU |
| Autocrat | | G-AHAW, G-AGXX, G-AGXU, |
| | | G-AGXS, G-AJAR, G-AJUH, |
| | | G-AJAB, G-AGXB |
| Auster V | | G-AJXC, G-AKXP, G-AKXR, |
| | | G-AKXS, G-AMNU |
| Aiglet Tr. | | G-AMUJ, G-AMUI |
| Auster Arrow | 0:10 | G-AJXZ |
| Percival Proctor | 124:00 | G-AGTF, G-AHTV, G-AKZN, |
| I, III & IV | | G-AKWE |
| Miles Gemini | 54:30 | G-AJZO, G-AJTB, G-AJWC, |
| | | G-AJOK, G-AKHC |
| Avro Anson XIX | | G-AGPG |
| Miles Messenger | 1:20 | G-AHUI, G-AKIN |
| DH(C) Chipmunk | | |
| T.10, 21, 22, 23 | 3225:50 | G-AKCS, G-AMMA, G-AMUC, |
| | | G-AMUD, G-AMUE, G-AMUF, |
| | | G-AMUG, G-AMUH, G-ARMG, |
| | | G-ARME, G-AOUN, G-AOUO, |
| | | G-AOUP, G-APSB, G-ARMF, |
| | | G-ATDP, G-AOZP, G-AOTZ, |
| | | G-AOJY, G-ARMD, G-ARMB, |
| | | G-ATEA, G-BFAX, G-AOZV, |
| | | G-AOTZ |
| Piper Cub Coupé | 0:05 | G-AFPP |
| Tipsy B. Srs 1 | 0:15 | G-AFRU |
| DH.85 Leopard Moth | 0:10 | G-ACRW |
| Dart Kitten | 0:20 | G-AEXT |
| Aeronca Chief | 0:10 | OO-TWT |
| Airspeed Consul | | G-AJXH, G-AJXG, G-AJXE, |
| | | G-AJXI |
| Miles M.18 | 0:50 | G-AHKY |
| Percival Prentice | 0:25 | |
| Cessna 140 | 0:15 | HB-CAV |
| Cessna 180 | 2:55 | HB-COZ, G-AXZO |
| Edgar-Percival EP.9 | 0:10 | G-AOZO |

| | | |
|---|---|---|
| Piper PA-23 Apache | 792:45 | G-APFV, G-ARJS, G-ARJT, G-ARJU, G-ARSV, G-ARJW, G-ARJX, G-ATMU, G-ASDG, G-ASDH, G-ATOA |
| Cessna 310 | 0:15 | |
| Miles Falcon Six | 0:10 | G-AECC |
| Piper PA-22 Tripacer | 0:15 | F-OBGZ |
| Piaggio P.166 | 0:15 | G-APSJ |
| Currie Wot | 0:15 | G-APWT |
| Druine Turbulent | 0:10 | G-APYZ |
| Piper PA-28 Cherokee 140 & 180 | 2337:10 | G-AVBA, G-AVBB, G-AVBC, G-AVBD, G-AVBE, G-AVBG, G-AVBH, G-AVBI, G-AVBJ, G-AVAX, G-AVAY, G-AVAZ, G-AVNN, G-AVNO, G-AVNM, G-AVNS, G-AVNN, G-AVNV, G-AVNW, G-AXZC, G-AXZD, G-AXZE, G-AYAR, G-AYEE, G-AYEF, G-AYAA, G-AVYO, G-AVFY |
| Cherokee Warrior | | G-BPCK |
| Thruxton Jackaroo | 0:10 | G-ANFY |
| Piper PA-23 Aztec 150 | 2:00 | G-AREE, G-ATBV, G-ASDH |
| Forney Aircoupe | 0:15 | G-ARHE |
| Saab Safir | 0:30 | G-ANOK |
| Beagle Airedale | 0:30 | G-ARXB |
| Piper PA-24 Comanche | 0:20 | G-ARFY |
| Beagle 206 | 1:05 | G-ASMK |
| Piper PA-30 Twin Comanche | 0:35 | G-ASRO |
| Beech Travelair | 1:30 | G-ASYV |
| Beechcraft Baron (B55, C55, D55) | 372:40 | G-AWAF, G-AWAG, G-AWAH, G-AWAI, G-AWAJ, G-AWAK, G-AWAL, G-AWAM, G-AWAN, G-AWAO, G-ATGR |
| Bölkow Junior | 0:15 | G-ATVB |
| Wassmer Baladou | 0:15 | G-ATSY |
| Cessna 172 | 117:45 | G-AWMU, G-AZKG, G-AXVX, G-BAEY, G-BGCR, G-BGNS |
| Beech Musketeer | 0:30 | G-AVDP |
| Piper PA-32 Cherokee Six | 0:20 | G-AVFU |

| | | |
|---|---|---|
| Beagle Pup 150 | 0:55 | G-AVLN |
| Glos. Airtourer | 2:30 | |
| Cessna 150 | 936:55 | G-BAEV, G-AYOZ, G-ARYP, G-BFLN, G-BBKB, G-AVGL, G-AYCF, G-BDNR, G-AYXV, G-AXRU |
| Beagle Pup 100 | 1:00 | G-AXDV |
| Robin DR.400 | 0:15 | G-BBCG |
| Cessna 177RG | 8:45 | G-AYSY, G-AYPF, G-BBXT |
| Cessna 152 | 3:15 | |

AS P2

| | | |
|---|---|---|
| Armstrong Whitworth Whitley V | 0:35 | |
| Avro Lancaster III | 4:45 | |
| DH.104 Dove | 7:20 | G-ANUS, G-ANUT, G-ANUU, G-ANUV, G-ANUW |
| Vickers Viscount 802 | 0:30 | G-APIM, G-AOHW |
| Vickers Vanguard | 1:25 | G-APES, G-APET |
| Boeing 707 | 0:10 | |
| Grob 109B | 2:00 | G-BMGR |

AS P3

| | | |
|---|---|---|
| Fairey Firefly T.Mk.1 | 0:20 | |
| Miles Student | 0:35 | G-APLK |
| Supermarine Spitfire VIII | 0:10 | G-AIDN |

AS PASSENGER (PREWAR)

| | |
|---|---|
| Short Scion | G-ADDV |
| Monospar | G-ACGI, G-ADVH |
| DH Dragon | G-AECZ |
| DH.60 Moth | G-EBVD |
| DH. Dragonfly | G-ADNA |
| Percival Gull | G-ADFA |

GLIDERS

| | |
|---|---|
| Kirby Cadet (P1) | 0:20 |
| Kirby Tutor (P1) | 0:20 |
| Grunau Baby (P1) | 0:05 |
| Kranich (P3) | 0:45 |
| Gen. Aircraft Hotspur (P2) | 0:10 |
| RS.28 (P2) | 0:55 |

| | |
|---|---|
| **TOTAL HOURS FLOWN:** | **16,411:30** |
| **TOTAL HOURS AS INSTRUCTOR:** | **12,370** |
| **TOTAL HOURS AS P1:** | **14,052** |

# APPENDIX 11

## AIRFIELDS LANDED AT

PREWAR:

Ramsgate
Manston
Hansey Green
Bekesbourne
Lympne
Swalecliffe
Broxbourne
Gravesend
West Malling
Shoreham
Wilmington
Exeter
Roborough

Woodley
Eastleigh
Le Zoute
Le Touquet
Hanworth
Redhill
Southend
Rochester
Maylands
Ipswich
Brooklands
Hatfield
Margate Front

WARTIME:

Yatesbury
Alton Barnes
Weston-super-Mare
South Cerney
Heston
Little Rissington
South Marston
Worthy Down
Hullavington
Peterborough
Sealand
Moreton-in-Marsh
Bibury
Long Newton
Babdown Farm
Wroughton
Watchfield
Boscombe Down
Upavon
Cranwell North
Cranwell South
Fulbeck
Southrop

Derby
Grantham
Kidlington
Windrush
Church Lawford
Luton
Henlow
Cambridge
Sywell
Whitney
Cottesmore
Cranfield
Clyffe Pypard
Andover
Wanborough
Bicester
Halton
Brize Norton
Kelmscott
Upper Heyford
Kemble
Colerne
Shellingford

Abingdon
Docking
Ansty
Bramcote
Booker
Hurn
Hendon
White Waltham
Harwell
Yeovil
Northolt
Staverton
Cranage
Stanton Harcourt
Chipping Warden
Chipping Norton
Shawbury
Thame
Wheaton Aston
Newton
Perton
Stradishall
Wrexham
Honiley
Condover
Warwick
Hinstock
Ternhill
Bridleway Gate
Halfpenny Green
Tilstock
Montford Bridge
Bratton
Worcester
Stretton
Defford
Dalcross
Thruxton
Greenham Common
Sleap
Rednal
Hinton-in-the-Hedges
Poulton

Wymeswold
Peplow
Jurby
Silverstone
Calveley
Wolverhampton
Bitteswell
Christchurch
Seighford
Lyneham
Shobdon
Westcott
Oakley
Grove
Warboys
Wyton
Graveley
Methwold
Bourn
Upwood
Little Staughton
Woodbridge
Wratting Common
Pershore
Ludham
Elmdon
Hams Hall
Henley
Waltham St. Lawrence
Sibson
Lords Bridge
Panshanger
Wattisham
Aston Down
Duxford
Mepal
Bircham Newton
Tuddenham
Feltwell
Farnham (field)
Waterbeach
Baginton

POSTWAR:

Croydon
Manea
Coltishall
Mildenhall
Castle Bromwich
York
Southsea
Barton
Ringway
Doncaster
Rearsby
Thornaby
Croft
Newmarket
Burtonwood
Honeydon
Birdbrock (field)
Hereford
Desford
Speke
Langham
Rougham (Bury)
Tollerton
Whitchurch
Elstree
Middle Wallop
Samlesbury
Squires Gate
Lille
Luxembourg
Prestwick
Leconfield
Liège
Turnhouse
Sherburn-in-Elmet
Topcliffe
Heathrow (London Airport)
Woolsington
Brough
Hawarden
Kenley
Somersham

Hamble
Gatwick
Yeadon
Thorney Island
Brockworth
Framlingham
Gransden Lodge
Fairoaks
Fiskerton
Deauville
Leavesden
Dalton
Somerton (Cowes)
Chepstow
Jersey
Coningsby
Spalding
Bognor
Oakington
Horsey Toll
Waddington
Hornchurch
Stoke Ferry
Tangmere
Marham
Skegness
Feltwell Fen (field)
Farcet
Wellesbourne Mountford
Llandow
Cardiff (Pengham Moors)
Carlisle (Kingstown)
Toussus-le-Noble
North Weald
Ambersham
Bintre (Sayers' Field)
Aldermaston
Redcar Racecourse
Keystone (Spiller's Field)
Lanark Racecourse
Boston
Old Sarum

Haydock Park Racecourse
Lee (field)
Filton
Hambledon
Downton (field)
Stansted
Bembridge
Gosport
Hastings (field)
Lyon (Bron)
Rome (Ciampino)
Malta (Luqa)
Cagliari (Elmas)
West Raynham
Sandown
Dunsfold
Bovingdon
Tarrant Rushton
Weston Zoyland
Stoney Cross
Silloth
Stapleford Tawney
Lulsgate
Old Warden
Rhoose
Alderney
Nutts Corner
St. Mary's (Scilly Isles)

Chilbolton
Lee-on-Solent
Swansea
Biggin Hill
Swanton Morley
Guernsey
Blackbushe
East Midlands (Castle
  Donington)
Goodwood
Ford
Lydd
Dublin
Compton Abbas
Ronaldsway
Shannon
Dinard
Leicester East
Norwich
Headcorn
Popham
Dunkeswell
Denham
Yeovilton
Farnborough
Land's End
Lasham

**TOTAL: 304**